TEPHIYLAH YHWH
"THE LORD'S PRAYER"

אָבִינוּ שֶׁבַּשָּׁמַיִם יִתְקַדֵשׁ שְׁמֶךָ, תָּבֹא מַלְכוּתֶךָ, יֵעָשֶׂה רְצוֹנְךָ כְּבַשָּׁמַיִם

AVINU SHAY-BA-SHAMAYIM, YIT-QADESH SHEM-KA, TABO MALKUT-KA, YAY'ASEH RETZON-KA. KE-BA-SHAMAYIM

גַם בָּאָרֶץ. תֶּן לָנוּ אֶת לֶחֶם צָרְכֵּנוּ הַיוֹם, וּמְחַל לָנוּ אֶת חוֹבוֹתֵינוּ כְּמוֹ

GAM BA-ARETZ. TAYN LANU ET LEKHEM TZARKENU HA-YOM, U'MEKHAL LANU ET KHOVOTAYNU KEMO

שֶׁגַם אֲנַחְנוּ מָחַלְנוּ לְחַיָּבֵינוּ. וְאַל תְּבִיאֵנוּ לִידֵי נִסָּיוֹן, אֶלָּא הַצִּילֵנוּ מִן

SHE-GAM ANAKHNU MAKHALNU LEKHAYA'VAYNU. W' AL TEVIAYNU LIDAY NISAYON, ELA HATZILAYNU MIN

הָרָע. כִּי שֶׁלְךָ הִיא הַמַּלְכוּת וְהַגְּבוּרָה וְהַתִּפְאֶרֶת לְעוֹלְמֵי עוֹלָמִים.

HA-RA. KI SHEL-KA HEE HA-MALKUT, W' HA-GAVURAH, W' HA-TIPHERAH L' OLMAY OLAMIM.

Shalom Brothers and Sisters. Here is YAHOWAH'S PRAYER translated from the original Hebrew/Aramaic Peshitta text. MattitYAHU (Matthew) 6:9-13.
HALLELUYAH!

H.I.S. WORD
Israelite Name Book &
Concordance

A MESSAGE FROM KHAI YASHUA PRESS

We are grateful for the support you've shown to Khai Yashua Press by purchasing this Bible translation. One of our goals for this "H.I.S. WORD Israelite Name Book & Concordance" is to highlight the original Hebraic faith of the Holy Bible and Apocrypha. We strive to reveal the hidden history and forgotten heritage and LANGUAGE to the Lost Tribes of Israel who were sold into slavery for their disobedience to Yahowah.

> DEUTERONOMY 28:68
> "AND YAHOWAH SHALL BRING THEE INTO EGYPT (BONDAGE) AGAIN WITH SHIPS (CARGO SLAVE SHIPS), by the way whereof I spake unto thee, Thou shalt see it no more again: AND THERE YE SHALL BE SOLD UNTO YOUR ENEMIES FOR BONDMEN AND BONDWOMEN, AND NO MAN SHALL BUY (REDEEM) YOU."

"H.I.S. WORD" clearly tells us (Hebrew Israelites) that we must return back to the covenant for our Father Yahowah to remember us and redeem/save us when Yashua returns.

> 2 CHRONICLES 7:14
> If my people, which are called by my name, shall humble themselves, and pray, and seek my face, and turn from their wicked ways; then will I hear from heaven, and will forgive their sin, and will heal their land.

Will you answer this question?... How can you turn back to the covenant if you have not read it ALL YOURSELF?

> REVELATIONS 10:8-9
> 8 And the voice which I heard from heaven spake unto me again, and said, Go and take the little book which is open in the hand of the angel which standeth upon the sea and upon the earth.
> 9 And I went unto the angel, and said unto him, Give me the little book. And he said unto me, Take it, and eat it up; and it shall make thy belly bitter, but it shall be in thy mouth sweet as honey.

Our MESHIAKH sent an angel to tell us to eat this scroll/book up!

We're excited to introduce to you several EXCLUSIVE FEATURES that help meet our goals of showcasing our History, Heritage and Language. The purpose of these EXCLUSIVE FEATURES is to highlight our original Hebraic faith. These EXCLUSIVE

FEATURES are designed to make "H.I.S. WORD" easier to study and understand!

> PROVERBS 4:7
> Wisdom is the principal thing; therefore get wisdom: and with all thy getting get understanding.

> 2 Timothy 2:15
> Study to shew thyself approved unto Elohim, a workman that needeth not to be ashamed, rightly dividing the word of truth.

These EXCLUSIVE FEATURES are only available in "H.I.S. WORD Hebrew Israelite Scriptures"!

Our prayer is that you will pick up "H.I.S. WORD" and read it all... because HIS WORDS are LIFE!

> PROVERBS 4:20-22
> My son, attend to my words; incline thine ear unto my sayings.
> Let them not depart from thine eyes; keep them in the midst of thine heart.
> For they are life unto those that find them, and health to all their flesh.

On the following pages we have explained all of the features and marked them with this marker so you can easily find the "EXCLUSIVE FEATURE" descriptions. **EF**

Also found on the following pages, in "About this translation," we ask that you pay attention to how important the Hebrew language is to our heritage. We can see that OUR HEBREW LANGUAGE is a unique identifier of our NATION, and it defines Our CULTURE and our CUSTOMS!

In closing, we hope that you will seek Yahowah's face, remember your HERITAGE and your LANGUAGE.

We have plans to make available many Hebrew language and study tools! We invite you to come visit our website to register your email so that you can stay informed. You will find us at HebrewIsraeliteScriptures.com

ABOUT THIS TRANSLATION

Mark 1:3 & Isaiah 40:3
"The voice of him that crieth in the wilderness, Prepare ye the way of YAHOWAH, make straight in the desert a highway for our Elohim."

We love, respect and recognize the power of the (1611) King James Bible. King James, who was a Hebrew Israelite himself, suffered assassination attempts because he defied the power of the Catholic Church by authorizing the translation of the Sacred Text into English for the masses.

The Catholic Church was unsuccessful at their assassination attempts so instead they sought to assassinate his personal character.

John 1:1
"In the beginning was the Word, and the Word was with Elohim, and the Word was Elohim."

The Old and New Testaments were written in the tongue in which it was inspired, (which the Apostles spoke). That language was Hebrew/ Aramaic.

Prologue to The Book of Sirach (Page 645)
"For the same things uttered in Hebrew, and translated into another tongue, have not the same force in them..."

We understand that according to Sirach some words when translated to another tongue, "have not the same force in them". So we have restored selected words (by careful comparison to the original Masoretic Hebrew Text & Aramaic Peshitta) with the intention of restoring the powerful force and meaning of the words from the Original Text and removing all of the Greek influences.

Here, Josephus Flavius, the Hebrew historian who lived in that time, proved that the Hellenic (Greek) culture was not accepted by Hebrew Israelites. They fiercely guarded

Hebrew/Aramaic which was the language of the people.

Wars of the Jews," Josephus in his preface, Section I
"I have proposed to myself for the sake of such as live under the Roman Government, to translate those books into the Greek tongue, which I formally composed in the LANGUAGE OF OUR COUNTRY..." (common Hebrew, otherwise known as Aramaic)."

The Antiquities of the Jews, Book 20, Chapter XI, Section 2
"I also have taken a great deal of pains to obtain the learning of the Greeks, and understand the elements of the Greek language, although I have so long accustomed myself to speak our own tongue, that I cannot pronounce the Greek with sufficient exactness, for our own nation DOES NOT ENCOURAGE THOSE THAT LEARN THE LANGUAGES OF MANY NATIONS...because they look upon this sort of accomplishment as common (profane)... there have yet hardly been so many as two or three that have succeeded (in learning Greek) therein who were immediately rewarded for their pains"

Furthermore, in the book of Maccabees we can see that when the wicked men of Yisra'el decided to make a covenant with the Greeks, we had "MUCH SORROW"

Maccabees 1:11
"In those days went there out of Yisra'el wicked men, who persuaded many, saying, Let us go and make a covenant with the heathen (Greeks) that are round about us: for since we departed from them we have had much sorrow."

The book of Maccabees also describes how the Greeks made laws stating that "all should be one people" and "many also of the children of Yisra'el consented to his "CUSTOMS". This is also true here in this captivity!

Maccabees 1:41- 49
"Moreover king Antiyokos wrote to his whole kingdom, that all should be one people, And every one should leave his laws: so all the heathen (Greeks) agreed according to the commandment of the king. Yea, many also of the children of Yisra'el consented to his CUSTOMS, and sacrificed unto idols, and profaned the sabbath. For the king had sent letters by messengers unto Yerushalem and the cities of Yehudah that they should follow the strange laws of the land, And forbid burnt offerings, and sacrifice, and drink offerings, in the temple; and that they should profane the sabbaths and festival days: And pollute the sanctuary and holy people: Set up altars, and groves, and chapels of idols, and sacrifice swine's flesh, and unclean beasts: That they should also leave their children uncircumcised, and make their souls abominable with all manner of uncleanness and profanation: TO THE END THEY MIGHT FORGET THE LAW, AND CHANGE ALL THE ORDINANCES."

Now we can see that the HEATHEN knows that when we take on their "CUSTOMS",

ABOUT THIS TRANSLATION

the end result is that we "FORGET THE LAW, AND CHANGE ALL THE ORDINANCES".

When you look up the definition of "CUSTOM" on Dictionary.com, here is what you find:

CUSTOM
- A habitual practice; the usual way of acting in given circumstances.
- Habits or usages collectively; convention.
- A practice so long established that it has the force of law.
- Such practices collectively.
- Sociology: a group pattern of habitual activity usually transmitted from one generation to another.

...When you look up the word "CULTURE" in the Oxford American Dictionary and Thesaurus, it says that the words "CUSTOMS" and "CULTURE" are synonymous or exactly the same. They define Culture as "the arts, customs and institutions of a nation, people, or group."

We can tie this all together by looking up the definition of the word "NATION". On Wikipedia.com, we can see that the HEBREW LANGUAGE is a unique identifier of our NATION, and it defines our CULTURE and our CUSTOMS!

A nation (from Latin: natio, "people, tribe, kin, genus, class, flock") is a large group or collective of people with common characteristics attributed to them — including LANGUAGE, traditions, mores (customs), habitus (habits), and ethnicity.

Again, we can see here in the book of Maccabees that Mattityahu said: "We will not hearken to the king's words, to go from our CUSTOMS"

Maccabees 2:17- 22
"Then answered the king's officers, and said to Mattityahu on this wise, Thou art a ruler, and an honourable and great man in this city, and strengthened with sons and brethren: Now therefore come thou first, and fulfil the king's commandment, like as all the heathen (Greeks) have done, yea, and the men of Yehudah also, and such as remain at Yerushalem: so shalt thou and thy house be in the number of the king's friends, and thou and thy children shall be honoured with silver and gold, and many rewards. Then Mattityahu answered and spake with a loud voice, Though all the Gentiles that are under the king's dominion obey him, and fall away every one from the CUSTOMS of their fathers, and give consent to his commandments: Yet will I and my sons and my brethren walk in the covenant of our fathers. Elohim forbid that we should forsake the commandments of Yahowah our Elohim and for us to break his covenant. WE WILL NOT HARKEN TO THE KING'S WORDS, TO GO FROM OUR CUSTOMS, either on the right hand, or the left.

TABLE OF CONTENTS

אנכי יהוה אלהיך אשר
הוצאתיך מארץ מצרים
מבית עבדים לא יהיה
לך אלהים אחרים על פני

לא תעשה־לך פסל וכל
תמונה אשר בשמים
ממעל ואשר בארץ
מתחת ואשר במים
מתחת לארץ

לא־תשתחוה להם ולא
תעבדם כי אנכי יהוה
אלהיך אל קנא פקד עון
אבת על־בנים על
שלשים ועל־רבעים
לשנאי: ועשה חסד
לאלפים לאהבי ולשמרי
מצותי:

לא תשא את־שם־יהוה

What Makes this Hebrew Israelite Concordance and Name Book Unique?

Did you know that the Hebrew Language is the first and most unique language spoken? What makes Hebrew so unique is that each letter has a meaning and numerical value. Each word also has a meaning, and when you put those meanings together it reveals prophetic messages. For example, if we look at the Name of the Father YAHOWAH, in Hebrew, it reveals a prophetic message about the Messiah, YAHOSHUA.

EACH HEBREW LETTER HAS A MEANING

YOD = ׳ = HAND

HEH = ה = BEHOLD

WAW = ׳ = NAIL

HEH = ה = BEHOLD

THE HIDDEN MEANING OF YAHOWAH'S NAME

IS:

BEHOLD THE HAND, BEHOLD THE NAIL!

ABOUT THIS CONCORDANCE

This Devine Mystery is Revealed in the Old and New Testaments.

PSALMS 22:16

"For dogs have compassed me: the assembly of the wicked have inclosed me: THEY PIERCED MY HANDS AND MY FEET."

ZACHARIAH 12:10

"And I will pour upon the house of Dawid, and upon the inhabitants of Yerushalem, the RUAKH of grace and of supplications: AND THEY SHALL LOOK UPON ME WHOM THEY HAVE PIERCED, AND THEY SHALL MOURN FOR HIM, AS ONE MOURNETH FOR HIS ONLY SON, and shall be in bitterness for him, as one that is in bitterness for HIS FIRSTBORN."

In this Hebrew (Ancient Paleo) Israelite Concordance and Name Book, you are provided the names, which are highlighted in purple from the Hebrew Israelite Scriptures, in their Hebrew pronunciation, Hebrew spelling, Ancient (Paleo) spelling, and its meanings. This Concordance is your premier resource to accompany the Hebrew Israelite Scriptures. Not only will you learn the names in Hebrew, but you will learn the meanings of the names which will add a deeper knowledge of the scriptures and the lives of our Patriarchs and Matriarchs.

John 8: 32
And ye shall know the truth, and the truth shall make you free.

As we are returning to our Hebraic Roots, many seek to obtain a Hebrew name. Look no further than this Hebrew Israelite Concordance and Name Book to choose a name for yourself and your children.

Psalms 127: 3
Lo, CHILDREN ARE AN HERITAGE OF YAHOWAH: and the fruit of the womb is his reward.

This Hebrew/Ancient (Paleo) Israelite Name Book and Concordance will provide you with a wealth of Hebrew names to choose from so that your children will walk in their heritage as a Hebrew Israelite.

For example, the name Nethan'EL (נתנאל) found in Numbers 1: 8 "Of Yissaskar; Nethan'EL the son of Tzuar", means Given of Elohim (God). What a powerful name for a Hebrew Israelite Prince.

"Then said I, Lo, I come: in the volume of the book it is written of Me, I delight to do thy will, O My ELOHIM" -Hebrews 10:7

For a daughter, the name Atarah (עטרה) found in 1 Chronicles 2: 26 "Yerakhme'EL had also another wife, whose name was Atarah; she was the mother of Onam", means Crowned. What a special name for a Hebrew Israelite Princess.

Just as the letters in the Name of YAHOWAH give the prophesy of YAHOSHUA, the Hebrew names in your family will tell a prophetic story as well when you remember that YAHOSHUA is in the volume of the book.

Psalms 40: 7
Then said I, Lo, I come: in the volume of the book it is written of me,

Hebrews 10: 7
Then said I, Lo, I come: in the volume of the book it is written of me, I delight to do thy will, O my ELOHIM.

One of the best examples of a prophecy being revealed is from the 12 Tribes as listed in Revelation 7.

Judah - Confession or praise of God
Reuben - Behold the Son
Gad - To overcome
Asher - Happy or blessed
Naphtali - To wrestle or striving with
Manasseh - Making to forget
Simeon - Hearing and obeying
Levi - Joined
Issachar - Reward
Zebulun - Habitation or dwelling place
Yoseph - He will add
Benjamin - Son of the right hand

The story that is revealed is.....

Behold the SON (YAHOSHUA) of Judah has overcome. He is blessed! He strove against forgetfulness and He has heard Levi. He is rewarded with a dwelling place. He is added to the Right Hand of The SON (of YAH)!

Using this Hebrew/Ancient (Paleo) Israelite Name Book and Concordance will enhance your learning and understanding of our Hebraic Language and Roots.

KHAI YASHUA ASSEMBLY

ISAIAH 36:16
Seek ye out of the book of YAHOWAH, and read: no one of these shall fail, none shall want her mate: for my mouth it hath commanded, and his RUAKH it hath gathered them.

Shalom w'ahavah (peace and love) to all! Welcome to Khai Yashua ministries. Our mission is to help the 12 Tribes of Israel arise from their slumber and return back to YAHOWAH.

Mar 2:11 I say unto thee, Arise, and take up thy bed, and go thy way into thine house.

We hope that through our new and innovative biblical teachings that you will experience exciting revelations that you never have before!

Mar 2:12 And immediately he arose, took up the bed, and went forth before them all; insomuch that they were all amazed, and glorified Elohim, saying, WE NEVER SAW IT ON THIS FASHION!

Author, Hebrew instructor and translator, bible teacher JediYah Melek has taught hundreds of thousands of people across the globe about the salvation and redemptive covenant of YASHUA HA' MESHIAKH.

Mar 2:13 And He went forth again by the sea side; and all the multitude resorted unto Him, AND HE TAUGHT THEM.

May The Ruakh HA' QADOSH open your heart to receive eternal life – the Life of YASHUA – KHAI YASHUA!!!

NOTES

HEBREW NAME PROPHECIES
(WRITTEN IN THE OLD TESTAMENT)
THE VOLUME OF THE BOOK

"Then said I, Lo, I come: in the volume of the book it is written of me" - **Psalms 40:7**

"אָז אָמַרְתִּי הִנֵּה־בָאתִי בִּמְגִלַּת־סֵפֶר

כָּתוּב עָלָי!"

"The bible is no more than a history book written by man. It's debatable to whether it's even accurate!" **This is the mindset of millions, maybe even billions of people.** The truth is, the bible is overfilled with hidden messages and prophecies. There is more than meets the eye when it come to the Bible. It is a book that is alive because it's relevant to the past, present, and the future. It is even an extreme weapon of mass destruction.

Hebrews 4:12 For the word of ELOHIM is quick, and powerful, and sharper than any twoedged sword, piercing even to the dividing asunder of soul and ruakh (spirit), and of the joints and marrow, and is a discerner of the thoughts and intents of the heart.

Colossians 1:26 Even the mystery which hath been hid from ages and from generations, but now is made man¬ifest to his saints

2 Timothy 3:16 All scripture is given by inspiration of ELOHIM, and is profitable for doctrine, for reproof, for cor¬rection, for instruction in righteousness:

There is an entire level of the Scriptures that millions and billions can't perceive because they fail to realize one thing. The entire Book is written about YAHOWAH and His Holy Son YAHOSHUA.

Psalms 40:7 Then said I, Lo, I come: in the volume of the book it is written of me.

He is perfect. There is nothing in Him that is impure, or not right. Therefore His words are life. In fact, even YAHOSHUA'S Name means salvation. He possesses all wisdom, knowledge, and understanding. There is no counsel whatsoever that YAHOWAH doesn't know about!

Ecclesiasticus 1:1 All wisdom cometh from YAHOWAH, and is with him for ever.

By knowing Him, we learn more and more about ourselves. Remember that we were created in His image. When you legitimately realize that the Book is Written about YAHOWAH and YAHOSHUA, your entire perspective of the Word will change completely.

BOOKS OF THE OLD TESTAMENT

GENESIS/BERESHITH: **IN THE BEGINNING**

EXODUS/SHEMOT: **NAME**

LEVITICUS/WAYIKRA: **WAS CALLED**

NUMBERS/BAMIDBAR: **IN THE WILDERNESS**

DEUTERONOMY/DEBARIM: **WORD**

JOSHUA/YAHOSHUA: **YAHOSHUA**

JUDGES/SHOFTIM: **JUDGE**

RUTH/RUTH: **FRIEND**

SAMUEL/SHEMUEL: **HEAR ELOHIM**

KINGS/MELEKIM: **KING**

CHRONICLES/DIBRAY HA'YAMIM: **TODAY'S MATTERS**

EZRA/EZRA: **HELP**

NEHEMIAH/NEKHEMYAH: **COMFORT OF YAH**

ESTHER/ESTHER: **STAR**

JOB/IYOB: **AFFLICTED**

PSALMS/TEHILIM: **PRAISE**

PROVERBS/MISHLAY: **PROVERBS**

ECCLESSIASTES/QOHELETH: **PREACHER**

SONG OF SOLOMON/SHIR SHELOMOH: **SONGS OF SHALOM**

ISAIAH/YESHAYAH: **YAH WILL SAVE**

JEREMIAH/YERAMYAH: **YAH WILL EXALT**

LAMENTATIONS/AEKAH: **CRY OUT**

EZEKIEL/YEKHEZQIEL: **GOD WILL STRENGTHEN**

DANIEL/DANIEL: **ELOHIM IS JUDGE**

HOSEA/HOSHEA: **DELIVERER**

JOEL/YOEL: **YAHOWAH ELOHIM**

AMOS/AMOS: **BURDEN**

OBADIAH/OBADYAH: **SERVE YAH**

JONAH/YONAH: **DOVE**

MICAH/MIKAH: **WHO IS LIKE**

NAHUM/NAKHUM: **COMFORTER**

HABAKKUK/KHABAQUQ: **EMBRACE**

ZEPHANIAH/ZEPHANYAH: **SECRETS OF YAH**

HAGGAI/KHAGGAI: **FEASTS**

ZECHARIAH/ZAKARYAH: **YAH WILL REMEMBER**

MALACHI/MALAKI: **MY ANGEL**

THE HIDDEN PROPHECY REVEALED

In the beginning a Name was called in the wilderness. YAHOSHUA is the Word. He is our judge and friend. ELOHIM will hear Him. He is King over today's matters. YAHOWAH is our Comforter and help. He is our Star. In His affliction He gave praises and preached proverbs. He sang songs of shalom. YAH OWAH will save Him. YAHOWAH will exalt Him. He will cry out, but YAHOWAH will stregthen Him. ELOHIM is Judge. YAHOWAH ELOHIM is Deliverer. The Servant of YAHOWAH carries our burdens. The Dove who is like The Comforter will embrace the Feasts and secrets of YAHOWAH. I YAHOWAH will remember My Angel.

ALEPH

Aleph is the first letter of the Hebrew alphabet. It is symbolized as 3 letters (2 Yods and 1 Waw) united in One. The numeric value of Aleph is 1 and also 1000. The symbolic meaning represents: strength, leadership and being first. YAHOSHUA is the "First and the Last." Aleph is typically a silent letter but it can also take on the sound of certain vowels.

HEBREW/ARAMAIC PRONUNCIATION	ENGLISH TRANSLATION	STRONG'S NUMBER	ANCIENT (PALEO) HEBREW	BIBLICAL HEBREW
ABIDAN	ABIDAN	H27	𐤉𐤃𐤁𐤀	אֲבִידָן

ab-ee-dawn';
From H1 and H1777; *father of judgment* (that is *judge*); *Abidan,* an Israelite: - Abidan.

| ABIGAYIL | ABIGAIL | H26 | 𐤋𐤉𐤂𐤁𐤀 | אֲבִיגַיִל |

ab-ee-gah'yil, ab-ee-gal';
From H1 and H1524; *father* (that is *source*) *of joy; Abigail* or *Abigal,* the name of two Israelitesses: - Abigal.

| ABIHUD | ABIHUD/ ABIUD | H31 | 𐤃𐤅𐤄𐤉𐤁𐤀 | אֲבִיהוּד |

ab-ee-hood';
From H1 and H1935; *father* (that is, *possessor*) *of renown; Abihud,* the name of two Israelites: - Abihud

| ABIYAH | ABIYAH | H29 | 𐤄𐤉𐤁𐤀 | אֲבִיָּה |

ab-ee-yaw', ab-ee-yaw'-hoo;
From H1 and H3050; YAHOWAH is my Father; *father* (that is *worshipper*) *of YAH; AbiYAH,* the name of several Israelite men and two Israelitesses: - Abiah, AbiYAH.

| ABNIQI | EUNICE | G2131 | 𐤉𐤒𐤍𐤁𐤀 | אַבְנִקִי |

yoo-nee'-kay;
From G2095 and G3529; *victorious;* Eunice, a Yehudith: - Eunice.

| ABRAHAM | ABRAHAM | H85 | 𐤌𐤄𐤓𐤁𐤀 | אַבְרָהָם |

ab-raw-hawm';
Contracted from H1 and an unused root (probably meaning *to be populous*); *father of a multitude; Abraham,* the later name of Abram: - Abraham.

HEBREW/ARAMAIC PRONUNCIATION	ENGLISH TRANSLATION	STRONG'S NUMBER	ANCIENT (PALEO) HEBREW	BIBLICAL HEBREW
ABRAM	ABRAM	H87	𐤌𐤓𐤁𐤀	אַבְרָם

ab-rawm';
Contracted from H48; high father; Abram, the original name of Abraham: - Abram.

| ADAH | ADAH | H5710 | 𐤄𐤃𐤏 | עָדָה |

aw-daw';
A primitive root; to *advance*, that is, *pass* on or *continue*; causatively to *remove*; specifically to *bedeck* (that is, bring an ornament upon): - adorn, deck (self), pass by, take away.

| ADAM | ADAM | H121 | 𐤌𐤃𐤀 | אָדָם |

aw-dawm';
The same as H120; *Adam*, the name of the first man, *ruddy*, that is, a *human being* (an individual or the species, *mankind*, etc.)

| ADDI | ADDI | H5716 | 𐤉𐤃𐤏 | עֲדִי |

ad-ee';
From H5710 in the sense of *trappings*; *finery*; generally an *outfit*; specifically a *headstall:* - X excellent, mouth, ornament.

| ADON ADONE | lord | H113 | 𐤍𐤅𐤃𐤀 | אָדוֹן |

aw-done', aw-done';
From an unused root (meaning to rule); sovereign, that is, controller (human or divine): - lord, master, owner. Compare also names beginning with "Adoni-"

| ADONAI | Lord | H136 | 𐤉𐤍𐤃𐤀 | אֲדֹנָי |

ad-o-noy';
An emphatic form of H113; the Lord (used as a proper name of Elohim only): - (my) Lord.

HEBREW/ARAMAIC PRONUNCIATION	ENGLISH TRANSLATION	STRONG'S NUMBER	ANCIENT (PALEO) HEBREW	BIBLICAL HEBREW
ADONI	my lord	H113	⁧ ⁩	אֲדֹנִי

aw-done', aw-done';
From an unused root (meaning to rule); sovereign, that is, controller (human or divine): - (my) lord, (my) master, (my) owner. Compare also names beginning with "Adoni-"

| ADONIYAH | ADONIYAH | H138 | ⁧ ⁩ | אֲדֹנִיָּה |

ad-o-nee-yaw';
YAHOWAH is my ADON (LORD). Son of Dawid

| AHALIBAMAH | AHOLIBAMAH | H173 | ⁧ ⁩ | אָהֳלִיבָמָה |

o"-hol-e-baw-maw';
From H168 and H1116; tent of (the) height; Oholibamah, a wife of Esau: - Aholibamah.

| AHARON | AARON | H175 | ⁧ ⁩ | אַהֲרוֹן |

a-har-one'
I will be exalted, lifted up; Aharon, the brother of Moses: - Aaron.

| AIYAH | AYAH | H344 | ⁧ ⁩ | אַיָּה |

ah-yaw'
Perhaps from H337; the screamer, that is, a hawk: - kite, vulture.

| AKHAB | AHAB | H256 | ⁧ ⁩ | אַחְאָב |

akh-awb;
from H251 and H1; brother (that is, friend) of (his) father; Achab, the name of a king of Israel and of a prophet at Babylon: - Ahab.

HEBREW/ARAMAIC PRONUNCIATION	ENGLISH TRANSLATION	STRONG'S NUMBER	ANCIENT (PALEO) HEBREW	BIBLICAL HEBREW
AKHAZ	AHAZ	H271	⟨paleo⟩	אָחָז

aw-khawz';
From H270; possessor; Achaz, the name of a Yehudim king and of a Yisraeli (Israelite) (Israelite): - Ahaz.

| AKHAZYAH | AHAZIAH | H274 | ⟨paleo⟩ | אֲחַזְיָה |

akh-az-yaw', akh-az-yaw'-hoo;
From H270 and H3050; YAH has seized; Achazyah, the name of a Yehudim and a Yisraeli (Israelite) (Israelite) king: - Ahaziah.

| AKHIEZER | AHIEZER | H295 | ⟨paleo⟩ | אֲחִיעֶזֶר |

akh-ee-eh'-zer;
From H251 and H5828; brother of help; Achiezer, the name of two Israelites: - Ahiezer.

| AKHIRA | AHIRA | H299 | ⟨paleo⟩ | אֲחִירַע |

akh-ee-rah';
From H251 and H7451; my brother is evil; brother of wrong; Achira, an Israelite: - Ahira.

| AKOR | ACHOR | H5911 | ⟨paleo⟩ | עכוֹר |

aw-kore';
From H5916; troubled; Akor, the name of a place in Palestine: - Achor.

| AKSAH'WEROSH | AHASUERUS | H325 | ⟨paleo⟩ | אֲחַשְׁוֵרוֹשׁ |

akh-ash-way-rosh';
Of Persian origin; Achashverosh (that is, Ahasuerus or Artaxerxes, but in this case Xerxes), the title (rather than name) of a Persian king: - Ahasuerus.

HEBREW/ARAMAIC PRONUNCIATION	ENGLISH TRANSLATION	STRONG'S NUMBER	ANCIENT (PALEO) HEBREW	BIBLICAL HEBREW
ALEKSANDROS	ALEXANDER	G223	‡የᎴᎮ⊿Ꮍ‡ Ɏ6⋉	אֲלֶכְסַנְדְּרוֹס

al-ex'-an-dros;
From the same as (the first part of) G220 and G435; man-defender; Alexander

HEBREW/ARAMAIC PRONUNCIATION	ENGLISH TRANSLATION	STRONG'S NUMBER	ANCIENT (PALEO) HEBREW	BIBLICAL HEBREW
ALMODAD	ALMODAD/ ELMODAM	H486	⊿⊿Ꮍ᎑6⋉	אַלְמוֹדָד

al-mo-dawd';
not measured; Almodad, a son of Joktan: - Almodad.

HEBREW/ARAMAIC PRONUNCIATION	ENGLISH TRANSLATION	STRONG'S NUMBER	ANCIENT (PALEO) HEBREW	BIBLICAL HEBREW
ALWAN	ALVAN/ ALIAN	H5935	ᎽᎽ6O	עַלְוָן

al-wawn', al-vawn'
From H5927; lofty; Alvan or Aljan, an Idumaean: - Alian, Alvan.

HEBREW/ARAMAIC PRONUNCIATION	ENGLISH TRANSLATION	STRONG'S NUMBER	ANCIENT (PALEO) HEBREW	BIBLICAL HEBREW
AMALEQ	AMALEK	H6002	ᕈ6ᎽO	עֲמָלֵק

am-aw-lake';
Valley dweller; Amalek, a descendant of Esaw; also his posterity and their country: - Amalek.

HEBREW/ARAMAIC PRONUNCIATION	ENGLISH TRANSLATION	STRONG'S NUMBER	ANCIENT (PALEO) HEBREW	BIBLICAL HEBREW
AMALEQIM	AMALEKITE(S)	H6003	ᎽᏉᕈ6ᎽO	עֲמָלֵקִי עֲמָלֵקִים

am-aw-lake';
valley dweller; Amalekite, descendants of Esau; also his posterity and their country: - Amalekites.

HEBREW/ARAMAIC PRONUNCIATION	ENGLISH TRANSLATION	STRONG'S NUMBER	ANCIENT (PALEO) HEBREW	BIBLICAL HEBREW
AMATZYAH	AMAZIAH	H558	ᎨᏉᎽᏙ⋉	אֲמַצְיָה

am-ats-yaw';
From H553 and H3050; strength of Yah; Amatsyah, the name of four Yisraeli (Israelite) (Israelite)m: - Amaziah.

A- INDEX

HEBREW/ARAMAIC PRONUNCIATION	ENGLISH TRANSLATION	STRONG'S NUMBER	ANCIENT (PALEO) HEBREW	BIBLICAL HEBREW
AMINADAB	AMMINADAB	H5992	9△ᗡᐯ𐤑O	עַמִּינָדָב

am-mee-naw-dawb';
From H5971 and H5068; my people are noble; *people of liberality*; *Amminadab*,
the name of four Israelites: - Amminadab.

HEBREW/ARAMAIC PRONUNCIATION	ENGLISH TRANSLATION	STRONG'S NUMBER	ANCIENT (PALEO) HEBREW	BIBLICAL HEBREW
AMMIHUD	AMMIHUD	H5989	△ᕽᗷᐯ𐤑O	עַמִּיהוּד

am-mee-hood';
From H5971 and H1935; *people of splendor*; *Ammihud*, the name of three
Israelites: - Ammihud.

HEBREW/ARAMAIC PRONUNCIATION	ENGLISH TRANSLATION	STRONG'S NUMBER	ANCIENT (PALEO) HEBREW	BIBLICAL HEBREW
AMMISHADDAI	AMMISHADDAI	H5996	ᐯ△ᗯᐯ𐤑O	עַמִּישַׁדָּי

am-mee-shad-dah'ee;
From H5971 and H7706; *people of* (the) *Almighty*; *Ammishaddai*, an Israelite: -
Ammishaddai.

HEBREW/ARAMAIC PRONUNCIATION	ENGLISH TRANSLATION	STRONG'S NUMBER	ANCIENT (PALEO) HEBREW	BIBLICAL HEBREW
AMMONIM	AMMONITE(S)	H5984	𐤑ᐯ 𐤑ᕽᐯO	עַמּוֹנִי עַמּוֹנִים

am-mone';
From H5971; *tribal*, that is, *inbred*; *Ammon*, a son of Lot; also his posterity and
their country: - Ammon, Ammonites.

HEBREW/ARAMAIC PRONUNCIATION	ENGLISH TRANSLATION	STRONG'S NUMBER	ANCIENT (PALEO) HEBREW	BIBLICAL HEBREW
AMON	AMON	H526	𐤑ᕽᐯO	עָמוֹן

aw-mone';
From H539, probably in the sense of *training*; *skilled*, that is, an architect (like
H542): - one brought up.

HEBREW/ARAMAIC PRONUNCIATION	ENGLISH TRANSLATION	STRONG'S NUMBER	ANCIENT (PALEO) HEBREW	BIBLICAL HEBREW
AMORAH	GOMORRAH	H6017	ᕽᕽᐯO	עֲמֹרָה

am-o-raw';
From H6014; a (ruined) *heap*; *Amorah*, a place in Palestine: - Gomorrah.

HEBREW/ARAMAIC PRONUNCIATION	ENGLISH TRANSLATION	STRONG'S NUMBER	ANCIENT (PALEO) HEBREW	BIBLICAL HEBREW
AMOTZ	AMOS	H531	ᛥᚲᚺᛟ	עָמוֹץ
aw-mohts'; From H553; *strong*; *Amots*, an Israelite: - Amoz.				
AMRAM	AMBRAM	H6019	ᛘᚲᚺᛟ	עַמְרָם
am-rawm'; Probably from H5971 and H7311; *high people*; *Amram*, the name of two Israelites: - Amram.				
ANAH	ANAH	H6034	ᚴᚺᛟ	עֲנָה
an-aw'; Probably form H6030; an *answer*; *Anah*, the name of two Edomites and one Edomitess: - Anah.				
ANAQIM	ANAKIM(S)	H6060	ᛘᚴᛊᚺᛟ	עֲנָק עֲנָקִים
aw-nawk'; From H6059; a necklace (as if strangling): - chain. A Canaanite(s)				
ANDRE	ANDREW	G406	ᚠᚴᛞᛀᛣ	אַנְדְּרִי
an-dreh'-as; From G435; manly; Andreas, a Yisraeli (Israelite) (Israelite): - Andrew.				
ANTYOKYA	ANTIOCH	G491	ᛤᚠ ᛉᚴᚠᛟᛣ	אַנְטְיוֹכְיָא
an-tee-okh-yoos'; From G490; driven against; an Antiochian or inhabitant of Antiochia: - of Antioch.				
AQAN	AKAN	H6130	ᛘᛊᛟ	עֲקָן

A- INDEX

HEBREW/ARAMAIC PRONUNCIATION	ENGLISH TRANSLATION	STRONG'S NUMBER	ANCIENT (PALEO) HEBREW	BIBLICAL HEBREW
From an unused root meaning to *twist*; *tortuous*; *Akan*, an Idumaean: - Akan. Compare H3292.				
ARAMIM	SYRIAN/ ARAMEAN(S) ASPIS	H758	𐤌𐤉𐤌𐤓𐤀	אֲרָם אֲרַמִּים
arawm'; From the same as H759; *the highland*; Aram or Syria, and its inhabitants; also the name of a son of Shem, a grandson of Nahor, and of a Yisraeli (Israelite) (Israelite): - Aram, Mesopotamia, Syria, Syrians.				
ARAM-NAHARAIM	MESOPOTAMIA	H763	𐤌𐤉𐤓𐤄𐤍-𐤌𐤓𐤀	אֲרַם–נַהֲרַיִם
ar-am' nah-har-ah'-yim; From H758 and the dual of H5104; *Aram of* (the) *two rivers* (Euphrates and Tigris) or Mesopotamia: - Aham-naharaim, Mesopotamia.				
ARAN	ARAN	H765	𐤍𐤓𐤀	אֲרָן
ar-awn' From H7442; *shout out*; *stridulous*; *Aran*, an Edomite: - Aran.				
ARBEL	JOBEL/ BETH ARBEL	H1009	𐤋𐤀𐤁𐤓𐤀	אַרְבֵאל בֵית–אַרְבֵאל
ar-bale'; From H1004 and H695 and H410; *Elohim (God)'s ambush*; *Beth Arbel*, a place in Palestine: - Beth-Arbel.				
ARETZ-AKHERETH ERETZ-AKHERETH	ARSARETH	NOT LISTED	𐤗𐤓𐤁𐤀-𐤑𐤓𐤀	אֶרֶץ–אֹחֶרֶת

HEBREW/ARAMAIC PRONUNCIATION	ENGLISH TRANSLATION	STRONG'S NUMBER	ANCIENT (PALEO) HEBREW	BIBLICAL HEBREW
From H776 and H312; another land; This is the land to which the ten tribes were deported (2 Esdras 13:45). It is described as "another land" lying a year and a half's journey beyond the river, i.e. the Euphrates. It probably answers to the Hebrew 'erets 'achereth (Deuteronomy 29:28). In Josephus' time the people were still believed to be there in countless numbers (Ant., XI, v, 2).				
ARPAKSHAD	ARPHAXAD	H775	⊿wУๅๆ⊀	אַרְפַּכְשַׁד
ar-pak-shad'; mouth gathers from the breast; *Arpakshad*, a son of Noah; also the region settled by him: - Arphaxad.				
ARTAKH'SHASHETH	ARTAXERXES	H783	⊀ XwwᗺXๅ⊀	אַרְתַּחְשַׁשְׁתָּא
ar-takh-shash-taw', ar-takh-shasht'; Of foreign origin; Artachshasta (or Artaxerxes), a title (rather than name) of several Persian kings: - Artaxerxes.				
ASA	ASA	H609	⊀ㅋ⊀	אָסָא
aw-saw'; healer; *Asa*, the name of a king and of a Levite: - Asa.				
ASHER	ASHER	H836	ๅw⊀	אָשֵׁר
aw-share'; From H833; *happy*; *Asher*, a son of Jacob, and the tribe descended from him, with its territory; also a place in Palestine: - Asher.				
ASHERIM	ASHERITE(S)	H843	ㅁㅋๅw⊀	אָשֵׁרִי אָשֵׁרִים

A- INDEX

HEBREW/ARAMAIC PRONUNCIATION	ENGLISH TRANSLATION	STRONG'S NUMBER	ANCIENT (PALEO) HEBREW	BIBLICAL HEBREW
Patronymic from H836; an Asherite (collectively) or descendant of Asher: happy - Asherites.				
ASSHUR ASSHURIM	ASSYRIAN(S)	H804	9ﬔwﾒ	אַשּׁוּר
ash-shoor', ash-shoor'; Apparently from H833 (in the sense of successful); Ashshur, the second son of Shem; also his descendants and the country occupied by them (that is, Assyria), its region and its empire: - Asshur, Assur, Assyria, Assyrians. See H838.				
ATHALYAH	ATHALIAH	H6271	ﾔﾔ6X0	עֲתַלְיָה
ath-al-yaw', ath-al-yaw'-hoo; From the same as H6270 and H3050; YAH has constrained; Athalyah, the name of an Israelitess and two Yisraeli (Israelite) (Israelite)m: - Athaliah.				
ATHINAS	ATHENS	G116	ﬠﾔﾔXﾒ	אַתִּינַס
ath-ay'-nahee; Plural of Athn (the goddess of wisdom, who was reputed to have founded the city); Athenae, the captital of Greece: - Athens.				
AZARYAH	AZARIAH	H5838	ﾔﾔﾗﾕ0	עֲזַרְיָה
az-ar-yaw', az-ar-yaw'-hoo; From H5826 and H3050; YAH has helped; Azaryah, the name of nineteen Yisraeli (Israelite) (Israelite)m: - Azariah.				
AZOR	AZUR/ AZZUR/ AZOR	H5809	9ﾕ0	עַזּוּר
az-zoor', az-zoor'; From <u>H5826</u>; *helpful; Azzur,* the name of three Israelites: - Azur, Azzur.				

ARI
(Lion)

HEBREW UNLOCKS THE BIBLE'S MYSTERIES

❝ The bible is no more than a history book written by man. It's debatable to whether it's even accurate." This is the mindset of millions, maybe even billions of people. The truth is, the bible is overfilled with hidden messages and prophecies. There is more than meets the eye when it come to the Bible. It is a book that is alive because it's relevant to the past, present, and the future.

Hebrews 4:12
For the word of ELOHIM is quick, and powerful, and sharper than any twoedged sword, piercing even to the dividing asunder of soul and ruakh, and of the joints and marrow, and is a discerner of the thoughts and intents of the heart.

There is an entire level of the Scriptures that millions and billions can't perceive because they fail to realize one thing. Hebrew is the key to unlocking the Bible's mysteries! Without a Hebraic understanding of H.I.S. WORD we cannot unlock the full potential of His RUAKH (Spirit).

Colossians 1:26
Even the mystery which hath been hid from ages and from generations, but now is made manifest to his saints

Since Hebrew is YAHOWAH'S language, it is also a language of mysteries. When you put the meanings of Hebrew names together, a message unfolds. An example of this is the meanings of the names of the 12 patriarchs put together. Their names prophesy about YAHOSHUA, our saviour. By combining the Hebrew names of a family together, you are revealing the purpose of the Hebrew family as a whole. You can also try this with your family. Connect the Hebrew meanings of each individual, and you will be amazed at the hidden message.

Our Hebrew name also reveals the destiny we must fulfill in YAHOWAH. For example, our forefather's name is Judah. Judah means praise. That was Judah's destiny! Since we are his descendants, it is also our duty to praise YAHOWAH. Everyone's gift, and duty on Earth is diverse, but it all points back to YAHOWAH. We are one body that reflects characteristics, and attributes of YAHOSHUA. Another example is Yokhanon (John). His name means YAHOWAH'S grace. Both grace, and praise are attributes of The Most High YAHOWAH! Don't you realize it? This is what the enemy is afraid of. When we come together, embrace or Hebrew names, and fulfill our Hebrew destinies, then we will be like a YAHOWAH on Earth. The enemy will be destroyed beyond repair!

Written by: YaqarYAH Bat JediYAH

BETH

Beth is the second letter of the Hebrew alphabet. The first word of the Hebrew Scriptures (Bereshit/Genesis) begins with Beth. The numeric value of Beth is 2. The symbolic meaning represents: Tent, Household and In/Inside. Beth symbolizes the idea of creation.

HEBREW/ARAMAIC PRONUNCIATION	ENGLISH TRANSLATION	STRONG'S NUMBER	ANCIENT (PALEO) HEBREW	BIBLICAL HEBREW
BABEL	BABYLON	H894	699	בָּבֶל
baw-bel'; From H1101; confusion; Babel (that is, Babylon), including Babylonia and the Babylonian empire: - Babel, Babylon.				
BALAQ	BALAK	H1111	𐤒𐤋𐤁	בָּלָק
baw-lawk'; From H1110; waster; Balak, a Moabitish king: - Balak.				
BAR-ABBA	BARABBAS	G912	𐤀𐤁𐤀-𐤓𐤁	בַּר־אַבָּא
bar-ab-bas'; Of Chaldee origin ([H1347] and G5 (Greek)); son of Abba; Bar-abbas, a Yisraeli (Israelite): - Barabbas.				
BAR-NABI	BARNABAS	G921	𐤍𐤁𐤍-𐤓𐤁	בַּר־נַבִי
bar-nab'-as; Of Chaldee origin [H1247] and [H5029]; son of Nabas (that is, prophecy); Barnabas, a Yisraeli (Israelite).				
BAR-TALMAI	BARTHOLOMEW	G924	𐤉𐤌𐤋𐤕-𐤓𐤁	בַּר־תַּלְמָי
bar-tim-ah'-yos; Of Chaldee origin [H1247] and [H2931]; son of Timaeus (or the unclean); Bartimaeus, a Yisraeli (Israelite): - Bartimus.				
BASMATH	BASHEMATH	H1315	𐤕𐤌𐤔𐤁	בָּשְׂמַת

HEBREW/ARAMAIC PRONUNCIATION	ENGLISH TRANSLATION	STRONG'S NUMBER	ANCIENT (PALEO) HEBREW	BIBLICAL HEBREW

HEBREW/ARAMAIC PRONUNCIATION	ENGLISH TRANSLATION	STRONG'S NUMBER	ANCIENT (PALEO) HEBREW	BIBLICAL HEBREW
bos-math'; Feminine of the second form of H1314; *fragrance;* smell, spice, sweet (odour); *Bosmath,* the name of a wife of Esau, and of a dughter of Solomon: - Bashemath, Basmath.				
BATZRAH	BOZRAH	H1223	ꓷꓥꚳꚶ	בָּצְרָה
bots-raw'; Feminine from H1219; an enclosure, that is, sheepfold: - Bozrah.				
BELIYA'AL	BELIAR/ BELIAL	H1100	60ꚳ69	בְּלִיַּעַל
bel-e-yah'-al; From H1097 and H3276; *without profit, worthlessness;* by extension *destruction, wickedness* (often in connection with H376, H802, H1121, etc.): - Belial, evil, naughty, ungodly (men), wicked.				
BENYAMIN	BENJAMIN	H1144	ꓬꚳꓬꚳꓬꓩ	בִּנְיָמִין
bin-yaw-mene'; From H1121 and H3225; son of (the) right hand; Binjamin, youngest son of Jacob; also the tribe descended from him, and its territory: - Benjamin.				
BENYAMINIM	BENJAMITE(S)	H1145	ꓬꚳꓬꚳꚳꚳ-ꓬꓩ	בֶּן־יְמִינִי בֶּן־יְמִינִים
ben-yem-ee-nee', ben-eesh' yem-ee-nee'; Multiple forms. Sometimes (with the article inserted); with H376 inserted (1Sa 9:1); son of a man of Jemini; or shorter (1Sa 9:4; Est 2:5); a man of Jemini; or (1Sa 20:1); more simply: a Jeminite; (plural patronymic from H1144; a Benjaminite, or descendant of Benjamin: son of the right hand - Benjamite, of Benjamin.				
BERNIQAH	BERNICE	G959	ꓱꚶꚳꓬꓩ	בֶּרְנִיקָה

HEBREW/ARAMAIC PRONUNCIATION	ENGLISH TRANSLATION	STRONG'S NUMBER	ANCIENT (PALEO) HEBREW	BIBLICAL HEBREW
ber-nee'-kay; From a provincial form of G5342 and G3529; victorious; Bernice, a member of the Herodian family: - Bernice.				
BETH'EL	BETHEL	H1008	𐤋𐤀-𐤕𐤉𐤁	בֵּית־אֵל
bayth-ale'; From H1004 and H410; house of Elohim; Beth-El, a place in Palestine: - Beth-el.				
BETH-HINI	BETHANY	G963	𐤉𐤍𐤉𐤄-𐤕𐤉𐤁	בֵּית־הִינִי
bay-than-ee'-ah; Of Chaldee origin; date house; Bethany, a place in Palestine: - Bethany.				
BETH-KHASDA	BETHESDA	G964	𐤀𐤃𐤎𐤇-𐤕𐤉𐤁	בֵּית־חַסְדָּא
bay-thes-dah'; Of Chaldee origin (compare [H1004] and [H2617]); house of kindness; Bethesda, a pool in Jerusalem: - Bethesda.				
BETHLEKHEM	BETHLEHEM	H1035	𐤌𐤇𐤋-𐤕𐤉𐤁	בֵּית־לֶחֶם
bayth leh'-khem; From H1004 and H3899; house of bread; Beth-Lechem, a place in Palestine: - Beth-lehem.				
BETH-PAGAY	BETH-PHAGE	G967	𐤉𐤂𐤐-𐤕𐤉𐤁	בֵּית־פַּגֵי
bayth-fag-ay'; Of Chaldee origin (compare [H1004] and [H6291]); fig house; Bethphage, a place in Palestine: - Bethphage.				
BETH-TZAIDAH	BETHSAIDA	G966	𐤄𐤃𐤉𐤑-𐤕𐤉𐤁	בֵּית־צֵידָה

B- INDEX

HEBREW/ARAMAIC PRONUNCIATION	ENGLISH TRANSLATION	STRONG'S NUMBER	ANCIENT (PALEO) HEBREW	BIBLICAL HEBREW
bayth-sahee-dah'; Of Chaldee origin (compare [H1004] and [H6719]); fishing house; Bethsaida, a place in Palestine: - Bethsaida.				
BETHUEL	BETHUEL	H1328	𐤋𐤀𐤅𐤕𐤁	בְּתוּאֵל
beth-oo-ale'; Apparently from the same as H1326 and H410; destroyed of Elohim; Bethuel, the name of a nephew of Abraham, and of a place in Palestine: - Bethuel. Compare H1329.				
BILAM	BALAAM	H1109	𐤌𐤏𐤋𐤁	בִּלְעָם
bil-awm'; Probably from H1077 and H5971; not (of the) people, that is, foreigner; Bilam, a Mesopotamian prophet; also a place in Palestine: - Balaam, Bileam.				
BILHAN	BILHAN	H1092	𐤍𐤄𐤋𐤁	בִּלְהָן
bil-hawn' From H1089; timid; to terrify; Bilhan, the name of an Edomite and of an Israelite: - Bilhan.				
BITHUNYA	BITHYNIA	G978	𐤀𐤉𐤍𐤅𐤕𐤉𐤁	בִּיתוּנִיָא
bee-thoo-nee'-ah; Of uncertain derivation; Bithynia, a region of Asia: - Bithynia.				
BOAZ	BOAZ/ BOOZ	H1162	𐤆𐤏𐤁	בֹּעַז
bo'-az; in him is strenngth; the ancestor of David; also the name of a pillar in front of the temple: - Boaz				

BETH
(House)

DALETH

Daleth (pronounced Dalet) is the fourth letter of the Hebrew alphabet. Daleth is also the Hebrew word for: door. The numerical value of Daleth is 4. It also symbolizes the idea of foundation.

HEBREW/ARAMAIC PRONUNCIATION	ENGLISH TRANSLATION	STRONG'S NUMBER	ANCIENT (PALEO) HEBREW	BIBLICAL HEBREW
DAMESEQ	DAMASCUS	H1834	ϙwצ⊿	דַּמֶּשֶׂק
dam-meh'-sek, doo-meh'-sek, dar-meh'-sek; Of foreign origin; Damascus, a city of Syria: - Damascus.				
DAN	DAN	H1835	ץ⊿	דָּן
dawn; From H1777; *judge*; *Dan*, one of the sons of Jacob; also the tribe descended from him, and its territory; likewise a place in Palestine colonized by them: - Dan.				
DANIEL	DANIEL	H1840	6א⅄ץ⊿	דָּנִיֵּאל
daw-nee-yale', daw-nee-ale' From H1835 and H410; *judge of Elohim (God)*; *Daniel* or *Danijel*, the name of two Israelites: - Daniel.				
DANIM	DANITE(S)	H1839	ץℽ⅄ץ⊿	דָּנִי דָּנִים
daw-nee'; Patronymic from H1835; a *Danite* (often collectively) or descendant (or inhabitant) of Dan: judge - Danites, of Dan.				
DARYAHWESH	DARIUS	H1867	wℽ⅄⅄9⊿	דָּרְיָוֶשׁ
daw-reh-yaw-vaysh'; Of Persian origin; *Darejavesh*, a title (rather than name) of several Persian kings: - Darius.				
DAWID	DAVID	H1732	⊿ℽ⅄	דָּוִד
daw-weed', daw-wid'; From the same as H1730; *loving*; *beloved*; *David*, the youngest son of Jesse: - David.				

D- INDEX

<table>
<tr><th>HEBREW/ARAMAIC PRONUNCIATION</th><th>ENGLISH TRANSLATION</th><th>STRONG'S NUMBER</th><th>ANCIENT (PALEO) HEBREW</th><th>BIBLICAL HEBREW</th></tr>
<tr><td>DESHONE</td><td>DISHON</td><td>H1788</td><td>𐤃𐤉𐤔𐤍</td><td>דִישֹׁן</td></tr>
<tr><td colspan="5">dee-shone'
From H1758; the leaper, mountain goat; that is, an antelope: - pygarg.</td></tr>
<tr><td>DISHAN</td><td>DISHAN</td><td>H1787</td><td>𐤃𐤉𐤔𐤍</td><td>דִישַׁן</td></tr>
<tr><td colspan="5">dee-shone'
From H1758; the leaper, mountain goat; that is, an antelope: - pygarg.</td></tr>
</table>

ד DAGIM (Fish)

THE 12 TRIBE PROPHECY

Genesis 49:1 And Ya'aqob called unto his sons, and said, Gather yourselves together, that I may tell you that which shall befall you in the last days.

2 Gather yourselves together, and hear, ye sons of Ya'aqob; and hearken unto Yisra'EL your father.

3 Reuben, thou art my firstborn, my might, and the beginning of my strength, the excellency of dignity, and the excellency of power:

4 Unstable as water, thou shalt not excel; because thou wentest up to thy father's bed; then defiledst thou it: he went up to my couch.

5 Shimon and Lewi are brethren; instruments of cruelty are in their habitations.

6 O my soul, come not thou into their secret; unto their assembly, mine honour, be not thou united: for in their anger they slew a man, and in their selfwill they digged down a wall.

7 Cursed be their anger, for it was fierce; and their wrath, for it was cruel: I will divide them in Ya'aqob, and scatter them in Yisra'EL.

8 Yehudah, thou art he whom thy brethren shall praise: thy hand shall be in the neck of thine enemies; thy father's children shall bow down before thee.

9 Yehudah is a lion's whelp: from the prey, my son, thou art gone up: he stooped down, he couched as a lion, and as an old lion; who shall rouse him up?

10 The sceptre shall not depart from Yehudah, nor a lawgiver from between his feet, until Shiloh come; and unto him shall the gathering of the people be.

11 Binding his foal unto the vine, and his ass's colt unto the choice vine; he washed his garments in wine, and his clothes in the blood of grapes:

12 His eyes shall be red with wine, and his teeth white with milk.

13 Zebulon shall dwell at the haven of the sea; and he shall be for an haven of ships; and his border shall be unto Tzidon (Zidon).

14 Yissaskar is a strong ass couching down between two burdens:

15 And he saw that rest was good, and the land that it was pleasant; and bowed his shoulder to bear, and became a servant unto tribute.

16 Dan shall judge his people, as one of the tribes of Yisra'EL.

17 Dan shall be a serpent by the way, an adder in the path, that biteth the horse heels, so that his rider shall fall backward.

18 I have waited for thy salvation, O YAHOWAH.

19 Gad, a troop shall overcome him: but he shall overcome at the last.

20 Out of Asher his bread shall be fat, and he shall yield royal dainties.

21 Naphtali is a hind let loose: he giveth goodly words.

22 Yoseph is a fruitful bough, even a fruitful bough by a well; whose branches run over the wall:

23 The archers have sorely grieved him, and shot at him, and hated him:

24 But his bow abode in strength, and the arms of his hands were made strong by the hands of the mighty ELOHIM of Ya'aqob; (from thence is the shepherd, the stone of Yisra'EL:)

25 Even by the ELOHIM of thy father, who shall help thee; and by the Almighty, who shall bless thee with blessings of heaven above, blessings of the deep that lieth under, blessings of the breasts, and of the womb:

26 The blessings of thy father have prevailed above the blessings of my progenitors unto the utmost bound of the everlasting hills: they shall be on the head of Yoseph, and on the crown of the head of him that was separate from his brethren.

27 Benyamin shall ravin as a wolf: in the morning he shall devour the prey, and at night he shall divide the spoil.

28 All these are the twelve tribes of Yisra'EL: and this is it that their father spake unto them, and blessed them; every one according to his blessing he blessed them.

REUBEN: Behold A SON	DAN: Judge
SIMEON: Obedient	GAD: Crowd
LEWI: Joined	ASHER: Happy
YEHUDAH: Praise	NAPHTALI: My Wrestling
ZEBULON: Habitation	YOSEPH: He Shall Add
YISSASKAR: Reward	BENYAMIN: Son of the Right Hand

THE 1st HIDDEN PROPHECY REVEALED

Behold the SON (YAHOSHUA) who we should hear and obey; join to and praise in our habitations. He will judge us if we crowd together to wrestle against Him. He is our reward and we are happy He has been added to the right hand (of the FATHER)!

REUBEN: Behold A SON	GAD: Crowd
SIMEON: Obedient	ASHER: Happy
YEHUDAH: Praise	NAPHTALI: My Wrestling
ZEBULON: Habitation	EPHRAYIM: Fruitful
YISSASKAR: Reward	MANASSHEH: Cause to Forget
DAN: Judge	BENYAMIN: Son of the Right Hand

THE 2nd HIDDEN PROPHECY REVEALED

Behold the SON (YAHOSHUA) who we should hear and obey. We should praise Him in our habitations. He will judge if we forget Him or come together in a crowd to wrestle against Him. He is our reward and we should be fruitful for Him. We are blessed He has been added to the right hand of the (FATHER)!

AYIN

Ayin is the sixteenth letter of the Hebrew alphabet. Ayin is also the Hebrew word for: eye. The numerical value of Ayin is 70. Like Aleph, Ayin is also a silent letter that can take on the sound of certain vowels. It is also the last letter in the Name of YAHOSHUA (יהושע).

HEBREW/ARAMAIC PRONUNCIATION	ENGLISH TRANSLATION	STRONG'S NUMBER	ANCIENT (PALEO) HEBREW	BIBLICAL HEBREW
EBAL	EBAL	H5858	𐤋𐤏𐤁𐤏	עֵיבָל

<table>
<tr><td colspan="5" align="center">

ay-bawl'
Perhaps from an unused root probably meaning to be *bald*; *bare*; *Ebal*, a mountain of Palestine: - Ebal.

</td></tr>
</table>

| EBHODIYAH | EUODIAS | G2136 | 𐤄𐤉𐤃𐤅𐤄𐤁𐤀 | אֲבְהוֹדִיָּה |

<table>
<tr><td colspan="5" align="center">

yoo-od-ee'-ah;
From the same as G2137; *fine travelling*; *Euodia*, a Messianic woman: - Euodias.

</td></tr>
</table>

| EBER | EBER/ HEBER | H5677 | 𐤏𐤁𐤏 | עֵבֶר |

<table>
<tr><td colspan="5" align="center">

ay'-ber;
region beyond; to *cross over*; *Eber*, the name of two patriarchs and four Israelites: - Eber, Heber.

</td></tr>
</table>

| EDEN/ EDNAH | EDEN/ EDNAH/ EUNA | H5730 | 𐤏𐤃𐤍 | עֵדֶן עֶדְנָה |

<table>
<tr><td colspan="5" align="center">

ay'-den, ed-naw';
From H5727; *pleasure*: - delicate, delight, pleasure. See also H1040.

</td></tr>
</table>

| EDOM | EDOM | H123 | 𐤌𐤅𐤃𐤀 | אֱדוֹם |

<table>
<tr><td colspan="5" align="center">

ed-ome', ed-ome';
From H122; *red* (see Gen 25:25); *Edom*, the elder twin-brother of Jacob; hence the region (Idumaea) occuped by him: - Edom, Edomites, Idumea.

</td></tr>
</table>

| EDOMIM | EDOMITE(S) | H130 | 𐤌𐤉𐤌𐤅𐤃𐤀 | אֱדֹמִי אֱדֹמִים |

HEBREW/ARAMAIC PRONUNCIATION	ENGLISH TRANSLATION	STRONG'S NUMBER	ANCIENT (PALEO) HEBREW	BIBLICAL HEBREW

ed-o-mee';
Patronymic from H123; an Edomite, or descendant from (or inhabitant of) Edom: - Edomite. See H726.

HEBREW/ARAMAIC PRONUNCIATION	ENGLISH TRANSLATION	STRONG'S NUMBER	ANCIENT (PALEO) HEBREW	BIBLICAL HEBREW
ELEAZAR	LAZARUS	H499	𐤀𐤋𐤏𐤆𐤓	אֶלְעָזָר

el-aw-zawr';
From H410 and H5826; Elohim (is) helper; Elazar, the name of seven Yisraelim (Israelites): - Eleazar.

HEBREW/ARAMAIC PRONUNCIATION	ENGLISH TRANSLATION	STRONG'S NUMBER	ANCIENT (PALEO) HEBREW	BIBLICAL HEBREW
ELI	HELI	H5927	𐤏𐤋𐤏	עֵלִי

ay-lee';
From H5927; lofty; Eli, an Israelitish high priest: - Eli.

HEBREW/ARAMAIC PRONUNCIATION	ENGLISH TRANSLATION	STRONG'S NUMBER	ANCIENT (PALEO) HEBREW	BIBLICAL HEBREW
ELIAB	ELIAB	H446	𐤀𐤋𐤉𐤀𐤁	אֱלִיאָב

el-ee-awb';
From H410 and H1; Elohim (God) of (his) father; Eliab, the name of six Israelites: - Eliab.

HEBREW/ARAMAIC PRONUNCIATION	ENGLISH TRANSLATION	STRONG'S NUMBER	ANCIENT (PALEO) HEBREW	BIBLICAL HEBREW
ELIASAPH	ELIASAPH	H460	𐤀𐤋𐤉𐤎𐤅	אֶלְיָסָף

el-yaw-sawf';
From H410 and H3254; Elohim (God) (is) gatherer; Eljasaph, the name of two Israelites: - Eliasaph.

HEBREW/ARAMAIC PRONUNCIATION	ENGLISH TRANSLATION	STRONG'S NUMBER	ANCIENT (PALEO) HEBREW	BIBLICAL HEBREW
ELIEZER	ELIEZER	H461	𐤀𐤋𐤉𐤏𐤆𐤓	אֱלִיעֶזֶר

el-ee-eh'-zer;
From H410 and H5828; my ELOHIM is help; Eliezer, the name of a Damascene and of ten Israelites: - Eliezer

HEBREW/ARAMAIC PRONUNCIATION	ENGLISH TRANSLATION	STRONG'S NUMBER	ANCIENT (PALEO) HEBREW	BIBLICAL HEBREW
ELIHUD	ELIHUD/ ELIUD	G1664	𐤀𐤋𐤉𐤄𐤅𐤃	אֱלִיהוּד

HEBREW/ARAMAIC PRONUNCIATION	ENGLISH TRANSLATION	STRONG'S NUMBER	ANCIENT (PALEO) HEBREW	BIBLICAL HEBREW
el-ee-ood'; Of Hebrew origin ([H410] and [H1935]); *ELOHIM of majesty*; *Eliud*, an Yisraeli (Israelite): - Eliud.				
ELIPHAZ	ELIPHAZ	H464	ⅠℲⱯ6X	אֱלִיפַז
el-ee-faz'; From H410 and H6337; my *Elohim (God) is gold*; *Eliphaz*, the name of one of Job's friends, and of a son of Esau: - Eliphaz.				
ELISHAMA	ELISHAMA	H476	oℲwℲ6X	אֱלִישָׁמָע
el-ee-shaw-maw'; From H410 and H8085; *Elohim (God) of hearing*; *Elishama*, the name of seven Israelites: - Elishama.				
ELI'TZUR	ELIZUR	H468	ⱯℲⱩℲ6X	אֱלִיצוּר
el-ee-tsoor'; From H410 and H6697; *Elohim (God) of* (the) *rock*; *Elitsur*, an Yisraeli (Israelite): - Elizur.				
ELIYAHU	ELIJAH	H452	ⱯℲℲ6X	אֵלִיָּהוּ
ay-lee-yaw', ay-lee-yaw'-hoo; From H410 and H3050; YAHOWAH is my Elohim, Elohim of YAHOWAH; Eliyah, the name of the famous prophet and of two other Yisraelim (Israelites): - Eliyah, Eliah.				
ELOHIM	Elohim (God)	H430	ℳℲ36X	אֱלֹהִים
el-o-heem'; Plural of H433; gods in the ordinary sense; but specifically used (in the plural thus, especially with the article) of the supreme Elohim; occasionally applied by way of deference to magistrates; and sometimes as a superlative: - angels, X exceeding, Elohim (gods) (-dess, -ly), X (very) great, judges, X mighty.				

HEBREW/ARAMAIC PRONUNCIATION	ENGLISH TRANSLATION	STRONG'S NUMBER	ANCIENT (PALEO) HEBREW	BIBLICAL HEBREW
ELON	ELON	H356	𐤉𐤋𐤏𐤀	אֵילוֹן

ay-lone',
From H352; *oakgrove*; strength; *Elon*, the name of a place in Palestine, and also of one Hittite, two Yisraeli (Israelite): - Elon.

| EL'YAQIM | ELIAKIM/ ELJAKIM | H471 | 𐤌𐤒𐤉𐤋𐤀 | אֶלְיָקִים |

el-yaw-keem';
From H410 and H6965; *Elohim (God) of raising*; *Eljakim*, the name of four Israelites: - Eliakim.

| EMORIM | AMORITE(S) | H567 | 𐤌𐤓𐤌𐤀 | אֱמֹרִי אֱמֹרִים |

em-o-ree';
Probably a patronymic from an unused name derived from H559 in the sense of publicity, that is, prominence; thus a mountaineer; an Emorite, one of the Canaanitish tribes: - Amorite.

| ENAN | ENAN | H5881 | 𐤍𐤍𐤏 | עֵינָן |

ay-nawn';
From H5869; *having eyes*; *Enan*, an Yisraeli (Israelite): - Enan. Compare H2704.

| ENOSH | ENOSH/ ENOS | H583 | 𐤔𐤍𐤀 | אֱנוֹשׁ |

en-ohsh';
mortal; man; *Enosh*, a son of *Seth:* - Enos.

| EPHESOS | EPHESUS | G2181 | 𐤎𐤅𐤎𐤍𐤀 | אֶפְסוֹס |

ef'-es-os;
Probably of foreign origin; Ephesus, a city of Asia Minor: - Ephesus.

HEBREW/ARAMAIC PRONUNCIATION	ENGLISH TRANSLATION	STRONG'S NUMBER	ANCIENT (PALEO) HEBREW	BIBLICAL HEBREW
EPHRATIM	EPHRAMITE(S)	H673	𐤌𐤏𐤕𐤀𐤓𐤐𐤀	אֶפְרָתִי אֶפְרָתִים

ef-rawth-ee';
Patrial from H672; an Ephrathite or an Ephraimite: double fruit, fruitfulness - Ephraimite, Ephrathite.

| EPHRAYIM | EPHRAIM | H669 | 𐤌𐤏𐤓𐤐𐤀 | אֶפְרַיִם |

ef-rah'-yim;
Dual of a masculine form of H672; double fruit; Ephrajim, a son of Joseph; also the tribe descended from him, and its territory: - Ephraim Ephraimites

| ER | ER | H6147 | 𐤓𐤏 | עֵר |

ayr;
From H5782; watchful; Er, the name of two Israelites: - Er.

| EREB | ARABIA | H6154 | 𐤁𐤓𐤏 | עֵרֶב |

ay'-reb, eh'-reb;
The second form used in 1Ki 10:15 with the article prefixed); from H6148; the web (or transverse threads of cloth); also a mixture, (or mongrel race): - Arabia, mingled people, mixed (multitude), woof.

| ESAW | ESAU | H6215 | 𐤅𐤔𐤏 | עֵשָׂו |

ay-saw';
Apparently a form of the passive participle of H6213 in the original sense of handling; rough (that is, sensibly felt); Esav, a son of Isaac, including his posterity: - Esau.

| ESHBAN | ESHBAN | H790 | 𐤍𐤁𐤔𐤀 | אֶשְׁבָּן |

HEBREW/ARAMAIC PRONUNCIATION	ENGLISH TRANSLATION	STRONG'S NUMBER	ANCIENT (PALEO) HEBREW	BIBLICAL HEBREW
esh-bawn' Probably from the same as H7644; *vigorous*; *Eshban*, an Idumaean: - Eshban.				
ESPARTA	SPARTANS/ LACEDEMONIAN	NOT LISTED	ⅎ𐤋ꟼ⊗ꟼ	סְפַרְטָה
a prominent city-state in ancient Greece. In antiquity the city-state was known as Lacedaemon (, Lakedaímn), while the name Sparta referred to its main settlement on the banks of the Eurotas River in Laconia, in south-eastern Peloponnese.[1] Around 650 BC, it rose to become the dominant military land-power in ancient Greece.				
ESTHER	ESTHER	H635	ꟼ×Ŧ⅄	אֶסְתֵּר
es-tare'; Of Persian derivation; star, Ester, the Yehudim heroine: - Esther.				
ETZER	EZER	H687	ꟼᛉ⅄	אֵצֶר
ay'-tser From H686; *treasure*; *Etser*, an Idumaean: - Ezer.				
EZRA	ESDRAS/ EZRA	H5834	ꟼꟼ⚏O	עֶזְרָה
ez-raw'; The same as H5833 help, aid; Ezrah, a Yisraeli: - Ezrah.				

ETZ
(Tree)

"Thus dwelt Esaw in mount Seir: Esaw is Edom."

ESAU AND JACOB: WHO'S WHO?

The Book of Genesis reveals the history of all nations and those nations are still here today. Each one has an origin in Genesis. The word "Genesis" means: genes or genealogy. "We cannot separate the nations of the Bible from the modern nations today. Understanding the Bible offers insight into who's who, yesterday and today. So, who is Esau?"

Esau is described as "red" in Genesis 25 and David is described as "ruddy" in I Samuel 16. The definitions are similar, leading us to consider that they may indeed be the same, or look the same. But since David is a descendant of Jacob/Israel and Esau is not, we know they cannot be of the same nation, which also physically means they do not look alike.

RED (Redneck) VS. RUDDY (Redbone)

1 Samuel 16:7

"But YAHOWAH said unto Shemu'EL, Look not on his countenance, or on the height of his stature; because I have refused him: for YAHOWAH seeth not as man seeth; for man looketh on the outward appearance, but YAHOWAH looketh on the heart...."

In I Samuel 16:7 we learn that with physical/carnal eyes, we can only see the outward appearance of others; but with spiritual eyes, we are able to see the heart of others. Take notice in 1 Samuel 16:11, the brothers of David were fierce, strong warriors. They were already fighting in Saul's army, so we know physically they were adequate, yet they were passed over by YAHOWAH.

Jesse replies to Samuel's question by answering, "There remaineth yet the youngest?" Think about the position of the youngest child. Using your spiritual eyes, what does this position mean, or what could it represent?

I Samuel 16 is a spiritual picture. David's brothers were all taller, stronger, and older than he was. He was the youngest, or the last one. We see many times in Scripture where Yah used thee last or the least of us. Read Matthew 19:36 and Matthew 20:16.

In I Samuel 16:12 We learn that David was "ruddy."

Strong's Word H132

The KJV translates Strong's H132 in the following manner: ruddy (2x), red (1x).

Outline of Biblical Usage: red, ruddy (of Esau as infant)

Strong's Definitions: admônîy, ad-mo-nee'; or (fully) admôwnîy ; from H119; reddish (of the hair or the complexion):—red, ruddy.

Was David an Edomite (European) or an Israelite?

Search "redbone African-American" in an online search for a visual of the characteristics of a ruddy Israelite.

Search "redneck European" in an online search for a visual of the characteristics of a ruddy Edomite.

They are both "red", but the Israelite on the left has melanin in his skin but the Edomite does not. It is obvious they do not share the same nation.

Being born in the land of Canaan, (a hot and dry climate) Esau's skin would have been continually exposed to the sun, consistently giving his skin a reddish hue. The Ashkenazi Jews (Europeans) living in the land of Israel today, have the second-highest rate of skin cancer in the world. If they belonged to that land, or were native to it, why are they diagnosed with skin cancer at this very high rate?

In Genesis 25:25, the author is clear to give a description of Esau's appearance, yet no description is given of Jacob/Israel. Why do you think that is? It goes without saying that Esau stood out. Edom (Europe) has a major feature that separates them (or sticks out) from all other people, the lack of melanin. They are the only group of people with no visible melanin

THE HISTORY OF ESAU

SEED OF THE SERPENT, SEED OF THE WOMAN

1 Samuel 16:7
> "And I [YAHOWAH] will put enmity between thee [serpent] and the woman, and between thy seed [serpent's seed] and her seed [woman's seed]; it shall bruise thy head, and thou shalt bruise his heel."

The seed of Satan (his children) and the seed of the woman (her children) is a prophecy from the beginning (Genesis 3) to teach us that there would be enmity between or amongst the two.

Enmity: The state or feeling of being actively opposed or hostile to someone or something.

In Genesis 25, we learn that though the twin brothers share the same biological parents, they would be born of two different nations. Think about why this is so.

Genesis 25:23
> "And YAHOWAH said unto her, Two nations are in thy womb, and two manner of people shall be separated from thy bowels; and the one people shall be stronger than the other people; and the elder shall serve the younger."

Rebekah had two different seeds, that is two different nations in her womb; Jacob who fathered the Israelites and Esau who fathered the Edomites (Genesis 36:9-36). One of them (and his descendants) preserves a righteous line and the other (and his descendants) preserves an evil (or serpent-like) line.

How do we know Jacob's seed is righteous? Jacob was renamed by YAHOWAH as Israel. YAH made a nation out of him called Israel, His chosen people. Israelites were personally chosen by YAH and He was their God. He also brought forth the Messiah, YAHOSHUA, through the nation of Israel. The seed of the serpent and the seed of the woman are not in the same line. It is clear that the Messiah did not come from the seed of the serpent, so He came from the righteous seed, or the chosen line, that is Jacob/Israel.

Genesis 25:25
> "And the first came out red, all over like an hairy garment; and they called his name Esaw (Esau).
> And after that came his brother out, and his hand took hold on Esaw's heel; and his name was called Ya'aqob (Jacob): and Yitzkhaq was threescore years old when she bare them."

Ya'aqob The Heel Grabber   Esaw The Red and Hairy

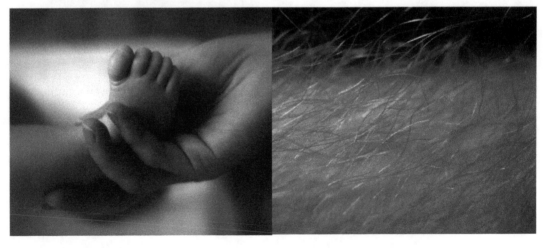

ESAU IS THE END OF THE WORLD

2 Esdras 6:7-10

"Then answered I and said, What shall be the parting asunder of the times? Or when shall be the end of the first, and the beginning of it that followeth?

And he said unto me, From Abraham unto Yitzkhaq, when Ya'aqob and Esau were born of him, Ya'aqob's hand held first the heel of Esau.

For Esaw (Esau) is the end of the world, and Ya'aqob (Jacob) is the beginning of it that followeth."

We learn through this passage that there's a battle or confrontation between the head and the heel of two different seeds/nations. It is not possible for Esau to be of the same nation as his brother, Israel. Esau is the end of the world, and Jacob grabbed onto the end of Esau (his heel). Once Esau's time is over, Jacob's dominion will follow after.

Which nation (or group of people)was under the heel of Esau (Edomites/Europeans) in Genesis 25? Which nation (or group of people)is under the heel of Esau currently? There's only one nation of people who are "under" or on the bottom in this present time. How can Europeans be Israel when they currently rule in power, own the wealth, and are "on top" as a people?

Let's survey which nation owns, rules, or possesses the power of our society today. Who's who?

- Who owns the media?
- Who owns construction?
- Who owns the music industry?
- Who owns real estate?
- Who owns the weapons?
- Who owns the government?

- Who owns the court system?
- Who owns agriculture?
- Who owns world trade?
- Who owns technology?
- Who owns the patents, trademarks?
- Who owned the slaves?

While Israelites are being stomped on and trodden under by Esau's heel, they will soon grab his heel (like Jacob did) to stop the enmity (opposition) of Esau, and he will be over. To grab Esau's heel, Jacob/Israel has to be on the bottom.

"The earth is given into the hand of the wicked: he covereth the faces of the judges thereof; if not, where, and who is he?" - Job 9:24

How can Esau be Israel?

How can Israel be Esau?

Europeans are not on the bottom right now, only Israel is. Israel is not on top right now, only Esau is. One cannot claim both. You're either first or last, either on top or on the bottom, either the oppressed or the oppressor.

THE HISTORY OF ESAU

ESAU THE HUNTER

Genesis 25:27

"And the boys grew: and Esaw (Esau) was a cunning hunter, a man of the field; and Ya'aqob (Jacob) was a perfect man, dwelling in tents."

One of the common practices for many Edomites is hunting for sport. Whether it is for wild game (deer in particular), fowl, fish or people, the descendants of Esau enjoy killing for sport.

Hunting is a cultural right of passage for Edomite males. With the earth under European rulership many species of animals (West African Black Rhinoceros, Pyrenean Ibex, Iberian wild goat, Passenger Pigeon, Quagga, Caribbean Monk Seal, Sea Mink, Tasmanian Tiger, Tecopa Pupfish, Javan Tiger, Great Auk, and the Bubal Hartebeest) have all been hunted to extinction. Many other species of wild life are endangered and their natural habitats are being destroyed.

"And the nations were angry, and thy wrath is come, and the time of the dead, that they should be judged... and shouldest destroy them which destroy the earth."

- Revelation 11:18

Genesis 36:1

"Now these are the generations of Esaw, who is Edom."

In Hebrew, Esau means "hairy" and Edom means "red." Re-read Genesis 36:1 and sub in these meanings:

H.I.S. WORD

1 Now these are the generations of Esaw, who is Edom.

2 Esaw took his wives of the daughters of Kena'an; Adah the daughter of Elon the Khittim, and Ahalibamah the daughter of Anah the daughter of Tzibon the Khiwwim;

3 And Basmath Yishma'EL's daughter, sister of Nebayoth.

4 And Adah bare to Esaw Eliphaz; and Basmath bare Reu'EL;

5 And Ahalibamah bare Yeush, and Yalam, and Qorakh: these are the sons of Esaw, which were born unto him in the land of Kena'an.

6 And Esaw took his wives, and his sons, and his daughters, and all the persons of his house, and his cattle, and all his beasts, and all his substance, which he had got in the land of Kena'an; and went into the country from the face of his brother Ya'aqob.

7 For their riches were more than that they might dwell together; and the land wherein they were strangers could not bear them because of their cattle.

8 Thus dwelt Esaw in mount Seir: Esaw is Edom.

9 And these are the generations of Esaw the father of the Edomim (Edomites) in mount Seir:

10 These are the names of Esaw's sons; Eliphaz the son of Adah the wife of Esaw, Reu'EL the son of Basmath the wife of Esaw.

11 And the sons of Eliphaz were Teman, Omar, Tzephi, and Gatam, and Qenaz.

12 And Timna was concubine to Eliphaz Esaw's son; and she bare to Eliphaz Amaleq (Amalek): these were the sons of Adah Esaw's wife.

13 And these are the sons of Reu'EL; Nakhath, and Zerakh, Shammah, and Mizzah: these were the sons of Basmath Esaw's wife.

14 And these were the sons of Ahalibamah, the daughter of Anah the daughter of Tzibon, Esaw's wife: and she bare to Esaw Yeush, and Yalam, and Qorakh.

15 These were dukes of the sons of Esaw: the sons of Eliphaz the firstborn son of Esaw; duke Teman, duke Omar, duke Tzephi, duke Qenaz,

16 Duke Qorakh, duke Gatam, and duke Amaleq: these are the dukes that came of Eliphaz in the land of Edom; these were the sons of Adah.

17 And these are the sons of Reu'EL Esaw's son; duke Nakhath, duke Zerakh, duke Shammah, duke Mizzah: these are the dukes that came of Reu'EL in the land of Edom; these are the sons of Basmath Esaw's wife.

18 And these are the sons of Ahalibamah Esaw's wife; duke Yeush, duke Yalam, duke Qorakh: these were the dukes that came of Ahalibamah the daughter of Anah, Esaw's wife.

19 These are the sons of Esaw, who is Edom, and these are their dukes.

20 These are the sons of Seir the Khorim, who inhabited the land; Lotan, and Shobal, and Tzibon, and Anah,

21 And Deshone, and Ezer, and Dishan: these are the dukes of the Khorim, the children of Seir in the land of Edom.

22 And the children of Lotan were Khori and Hemam; and Lotan's sister was Timna.

23 And the children of Shobal were these; Alwan, and Manakhath, and Ebal, Shepho, and Onam.

24 And these are the children of Tzibon; both Aiyah, and Anah: this was that Anah that found the mules in the wilderness, as he fed the asses of Tzibon his father.

25 And the children of Anah were these; Deshone, and Ahalibamah the daughter of Anah.

26 And these are the children of Deshone; Khemdan, and Eshban, and Yithran, and Keran.

27 The children of Ezer are these; Bilhan, and Za'awan, and Aqan.

28 The children of Dishan are these; Uz, and Aran.

ESAU THE HAIRY GOAT

Read Genesis 36:8, 20

Seir: Hairy goat, he goat, hairy, shaggy, a demon-possessed goat-like, Pan

Seir is a Hebrew idiom for the he-goat/human hybrid devil that is generally worshipped in the occult by means of an upside down pentagram. The demon of Mt. Seir is also refered to as the "god of war."

Horite: Cave dweller

The term "Horite/Horim" means: cave dweller. Cave dwellers are commonly refered to as: Caucasian. Edomites today are the Caucasian race.

ESAW AND HIS DESCENDANTS

ESAW/ESAU: HAIRY	SHAMMAH: HORROR
EDOM: RED	MIZZAH: FEAR
KENA'AN: HUMILIATED	SEIR: GOAT DEMON
ADAH: TO ADVANCE	KHORIM: CAVE DWELLER
ELON: STRENGTH	LOTAN: A COVERING
KHITTIM: TERROR	DESHONE: MOUNTAIN GOAT
AHALIBAMAH: MY TENT IS ELEVATED	ETZER: TREASURE
ANAH: ANSWER	DISHAN: MOUNTAIN GOAT
TZIBON: DYE	KHORI: CAVE DWELLER
KHIWWIM: VILLAGER	HEMAM: RAGING
BASMATH: FRAGRANCE	TIMNA: RESTRAINT
YISHMA'EL: ELOHIM WILL HEAR	SHOBAL: OVERFLOWING
NEBAYOTH: FLOURISH	ALWAN: LOFTY
ELIPHAZ: MY GOD IS GOLD	MANAKHATH: REST
REU'EL: GOD IS MY FRIEND	EBAL: BALD/BARE
YEUSH: HASTY	SHEPHO: BARE
YALAM: OCCULT	ONAM: STRONG
QORAKH: COLD	AIYAH: VULTURE
TEMAN: SOUTH	KHEMDAN: DELIGHT IN
OMAR: SPEAKER	ESHBAN: GROWTH
TZEPHO: OBSERVANT	YITHRAN: EXCELLENT
GATAM: A BURNT VALLEY	KERAN: HARP
QENAZ: A HUNTER	ZA'AWAN: DISQUIET
TIMNA: TO HOLD BACK	BILHAN: TERRIFY
AMALEQ: VALLEY DWELLER	AQAN: TORTURE
NAKHATH: REST OF DEATH	UTZ: CONSULT
ZERAKH: RISING LIGHT	ARAN: SHOUT

Petra: Mount Seir

THE HIDDEN PROPHECY REVEALED

1. Esaw (Esau) is hairy and red.
2. Esaw will be humiliated. He will advance in terror. He answers to his dyed tent elevated in his village.
3. His elohim has heard his fragrance and he flourished.
4. Esaw will advance. Gold is his elohim (god). He befriends his elohim with spices.
5. He elevated his tent in haste. The Occult has made him cold. Esaw will be humiliated.
6. Esaw will be humiliated by his brother Ya'aqob.
7. (No names listed.)
8. Esaw is the Goat Demon. Esaw is Edom.
9. Esaw and the Edomim are Goat Demons.
10. Esaw's elohim is gold. Esaw will advance. He befriends his elohim with spices.
11. His elohim is gold from the south. He is an observant speaker. A hunter from the burnt valley.
12. Esaw will withhold his elohim of gold. Amaleq's elohim is gold. He will advance with Esaw.
13. He is a friend to his elohim who rests in death! His light will rise in horror and fear. This is Esaw's fragrance.
14. Esaw answers to his elevated dyed tent. Esaw hastened into the Occult. He is cold.
15. Esaw's elohim is gold. Esaw is an observant speaker and hunter from the south.

16. Amaleq is cold from the burnt valley. Gold is his elohim. Esaw will advance.

17. Esaw is a friend to his elohim resting in death. His light will rise in horror and fear. Edom is a friend to his elohim. The fragrance of Esaw.

18. Esaw's tent was elevated in haste by the Occult. He is cold. Esaw answers to his elevated tent.

19. Esaw is red.

20. He answers to the cave dwelling Goat Demon. His covering is overflowing in diverse colors.

21. The Mountain Goat is his treasure. The cave dwelling Mountain Goat, the Goat Demon of Edom.

22. The cave dweller is covered in rage. His covering is restrained.

23. He overflows. He loftiness is made bare. His strength is made bare.

24. He answers to the vulture of diverse colors. An answer from one in diverse colors.

25. He answers to the Mountain Goat whose tent is elevated. He answers to him.

26. He takes pleasure in the Mountain Goat. He plays the harp with exceeding vigor.

27. He tortures and vexes with the treasures of terror.

28. He consults and rejoices in the Mountain Goat.

ESAU & THE MUSIC INDUSTRY (THE HARP)

The secret prophecy in Esau's genealogy continuously makes reference to the "Mountain Goat" and the "Goat Demon". The spiritual meaning behind this is Esau's worldly influence through the Satyr (half-goat/half-human) gods of the music and entertainment industries.

In order to attain worldly success in these industries, a blood sacrifice is required to the Goat of Mendes (Azazel: Leviticus 16:8, 10, 26). This demon is depicted as half-human and half-goat, having both male and female features. Satanic rituals are performed which usually include inverted pentagram symbolism to represent the face of the scape goat. When elite entertainers reach the height of their careers they are given a star on the Hollywood walk of Fame. This ceremony is performed on top of a pentagram to symbolize their demonic covenant with Satan.

YAHOSHUA classifies Israelites who believe in Him as "sheep". Those who do not He calls "goats". This is a clear reference to Azazel (the Satyr Goat Demon of Mendes) who uses sorcery in the form of entertainment to lead souls directly to hell.

"But the goat, on which the lot fell to be the scapegoat, shall be presented alive before YAHOWAH, to make an atonement with him, and to let him go to Azazel into the wilderness.?" - Lev 16:10

The Bible prophesied that in the last days Edomites (Romans/Greeks) would destroy Jerusalem and then sell the true Israelites into slavery (Obad 1:10-14/Joel 3:6-8).

In the book of Revelation YAHOSHUA named false "Jews" the Synagogue of Satan.

"I know the blasphemy of them which say they are Yehudim (Jews), and are not, but are the Congregation (Synagogue) of Satan." - Rev 2:9

"Behold, I will make them of the Congregation (Synagogue) of Satan, which say they are Yehudim (Jews), and are not, but do lie; behold, I will make them to come and worship before thy feet, and to know that I have loved thee." - Rev 3:9

BLOOD SACRIFICE & RAW MEAT

"Lest there be any fornicator, or profane person, as Esaw, who for one morsel of meat sold his birthright. For ye know how that afterward, when he would have inherited the blessing, he was rejected: for he found no place of repentance, though he sought it carefully with tears." - Hebrews 12:16-17

In the story of Jacob and Esau a very pivotal moment took place when Esau sold his birthright for red pottage (Gen 25:30-34). The birthright that Esau was set to inherit was the Torah and the Kingdom of Heaven.

The ultimate manifestation of this birthright was YAHOSHUA being born to shed His blood for the redemption of sin. When Esau sold this birthright he blasphemed The RUAKH HA' QODESH (The Holy Spirit). Hebrews 12:17 states that "For ye know how that afterward, when he would have inherited the blessing, he was rejected: for he found no place of repentance, though he sought it carefully with tears."

Since there was no repentance for this particular sin we know that blasphemy against YAH was committed. YAHOSHUA said that every kind of sin can be forgiven except for "him that blasphemeth against the RUAKH HA' QODESH it shall not be forgiven"(Luke 12:10).

This sale of Esau's birthright proves that he actually sold his soul to the Devil. Esau rejected the blood of YAHOSHUA and in His place ate the red (bloody) meat that most Edomites continue to eat to this day.

"And whatsoever man there be of the house of Yisra'EL, or of the strangers that sojourn among you, that eateth any manner of blood; I will even set my face against that soul that eateth blood, and will cut him off from among his people." - Leviticus 17:10

"And the boys grew: and Esaw was a cunning hunter, a man of the field..." - Genesis 25:27

GIMEL

Gimel is the third letter of the Hebrew alphabet. As a word, Gimel means: camel. The numeric value of Gimel is three. The symobolic meaning of Gimel is represented by wealth or as a rich man.

HEBREW/ARAMAIC PRONUNCIATION	ENGLISH TRANSLATION	STRONG'S NUMBER	ANCIENT (PALEO) HEBREW	BIBLICAL HEBREW
GAD	GAD	H1410	⟁⟍	גָּד

gawd;
From H1464; *Gad,* troop; fortune; a son of Jacob, including his tribe and its territory; also a prophet: - Gad.

| GADIM | GADITE(S) | H1425 | ⟋⟍⟍⟁⟍ | גָּדִי
גָּדִים |

gaw-dee';
Patronymic from H1410; a Gadite (collectively) or descendant of Gad: invade, overcome - Gadites, children of Gad.

| GADRIYIM | GADARENES | G1046 | ⟋⟍⟍⟍⟁⟍ | גַּדְרִים |

gad-ar-ay-nos';
From Gadara (a town East of the Jordan); a Gadarene or inhabitant of Gadara: - Gadarene.

| GALATYA | GALATIA | G1054 | ⟋⟍⟍⟍⟍ | גַּלְטִיָא |

gal-at-ee-kos';
From G1053; Galatic or relating to Galatia: - of Galatia.

| GALILAH | GALILEE | H1551 | ⟋⟍⟍⟍ | גְּלִילָה |

gaw-leel', gaw-lee-law;
The same as H1550; a circle (with the article); Galil (as a special circuit) in the North of Palestine: - Galilee.

| GAMLIEL | GAMALIEL/ GAMLIEL | H1583 | ⟋⟍⟍⟍⟍ | גַּמְלִיאֵל |

gam-lee-ale';
From H1580 and H410; *reward of Elohim (God); Gamliel,* an Israelite: - Gamaliel.

HEBREW/ARAMAIC PRONUNCIATION	ENGLISH TRANSLATION	STRONG'S NUMBER	ANCIENT (PALEO) HEBREW	BIBLICAL HEBREW
GATAM	GATAM	H1609	𐤌𐤀𐤏𐤂	גַּעְתָּם

gah-tawm'
a burnt valley; *Gatam*, an Edomite: - Gatam.

| GATH-SHEMANAY | GETHSEMANE | G1068 | 𐤉𐤍𐤌𐤔-𐤕𐤂 | גַּת־שְׁמָנֵי |

gheth-say-man-ay';
Of Chaldee origin (compare [H1660] and [H8081]); oil press, wine press; Gethsemane, a garden near Jerusalem: - Gethsemane.

| GERSHON | GERSHON/ GERSAM | H1648 | 𐤍𐤅𐤔𐤓𐤂 | גֵּרְשׁוֹן |

gay-resh-one', gay-resh-ome';
From H1644; a *refugee*; *Gereshon* or *Gereshom*, an Israelite: - Gershon, Gershom.

| GERSHONIM | GERSHONITE(S) | H1649 | 𐤉𐤍𐤅𐤔𐤓𐤂 | גֵּרְשֻׁנִי
גֵּרְשֻׁנִים |

gay-resh-one', gay-resh-ome';
From H1644; a refugee; Gereshon or Gereshom, a Yisraeli (Israelite): - Gershon, Gershom.

| GIBAH | GIBEAH | H1390 | 𐤄𐤏𐤁𐤂 | גִּבְעָה |

ghib-aw';
The same as H1389; Gibah; the name of three places in Palestine: - Gibeah, the hill, little hill.

| GIBON | GIBEON | H1391 | 𐤍𐤅𐤏𐤁𐤂 | גִּבְעוֹן |

ghib-ohn';
From the same as H1387; hilly; Gibon, a place in Palestine: - Gibeon.

HEBREW/ARAMAIC PRONUNCIATION	ENGLISH TRANSLATION	STRONG'S NUMBER	ANCIENT (PALEO) HEBREW	BIBLICAL HEBREW
GIDEONI	GIDEONI	H1441	✔𝓎𝒪△𝟙	גִּדְעֹנִי

ghid-o-nee';
From H1438; *warlike* (compare H1439); *Gidoni*, an Israelite: - Gideoni.

| GIL'ADIM | GILEADITE(S) | H1569 | 𝓎✔△0𝟞𝟙 | גִּלְעָדִי
גִּלְעָדִים |

ghil-aw-dee';
Patronymic from H1568; a Giladite or descendant of Gilad: heap of testimony - Gileadite.

| GINESAR | GENNESARET | G1082 | 𝟙╪✔𝓎𝟙 | גִּנֵּיסָר |

ghen-nay-sar-et';
harp; harp shaped;(compare [H3672]); Gennesaret (that is, Kinnereth), a lake and plain in Palestine: - Gennesaret.

| GULGOLETH | GOLGATHA/ CALVARY | H1538 | ⚔✗𝟞𝟙𝟞𝟙 | גֻּלְגֹּלְתָּא |

gul-go'-leth;
By reduplication from H1556; a skull (as round); by implication a head (in enumeration of persons): - head, every man, poll, skull.

HEH

Heh is the fifth letter of the Hebrew alphabet and the second letter in the Names of YAH (יה), YAHOWAH (יהוה) and YAHOSHUA (יהושע). Heh used as a prefix denotes the word: the (as a definite article). The symbolic meaning of Heh represents extended arms (in praise), to behold/look and a window. The numeric value is 5.

HEBREW/ARAMAIC PRONUNCIATION	ENGLISH TRANSLATION	STRONG'S NUMBER	ANCIENT (PALEO) HEBREW	BIBLICAL HEBREW
HARMEH	HERMES	G2060	₣ꟿꟼꟼ	הֶרְמָס

her-mace';
to *utter*, that is, *speak* or *say*: - call, say, speak (of), tell.; Hermes, the name of the messenger of the Greek deities; also of a Messianic: - Hermes, Mercury.

| HAYLEL | LUCIFER | H1966 | 𝟞𝟞𝟜𝟛 | הֵילֵל |

hay-lale';
From H1984 (in the sense of brightness); the morning star: - lucifer.

| HEBEL | ABEL | H1892 | 𝟞𝟜𝟛 | הֶבֶל |

From H1891;
emptiness or vanity; figuratively something transitory and unsatisfactory; often used as an adverb: -   X altogether, vain, vanity. The son of Adam.

| HELI* ELI | HELI | H5927 | 𝟜𝟞0 | עֲלִי |

ay-lee';
From H5927; *lofty*; Eli, an Israelitish high priest: - Eli.

| HODU | INDIA | H1912 | 𝟜𝟛 | הֹדוּ |

ho'-doo;
Of foreign origin; Hodu (that is, Hindustan): - India.

| HORODYAH | HERODIAS | G2266 | 𝟛𝟜𝟜𝟜𝟜𝟛 | הוֹרוֹדִיָה |

hay-ro-dee-as';
From G2264; Herodias, heroic, a woman of the Herodian family: - Herodias.

| ISHQERIOT | ISCARIOT | G2469 | ✗𝟜𝟜𝟜𝟜-𝟜𝟜✗ | אִישׁ־קְרִיּוֹת |

HEBREW/ARAMAIC PRONUNCIATION	ENGLISH TRANSLATION	STRONG'S NUMBER	ANCIENT (PALEO) HEBREW	BIBLICAL HEBREW
Of Hebrew origin (man [H377] and [H7149] to *light upon*, befall, bring, come (to pass unto); causatively to *bring about*;); inhabitants of Kerioth; Iscariotes (that is, Keriothite), an epithet of Judas (Yehudah) the traitor: - Iscariot.				
ITALYA	ITALY	G2482	‌	אִיטַלְיָא
ee-tal-ee'-ah; Probably of foreign origin; Italia, a region of Europe: - Italy.				
ITAMAR	ITHAMAR	H385	‌	אִיתָמָר
eeth-aw-mawr'; From H339 and H8558; coast of the palm tree; Ithamar, a son of Aaron: - Ithamar.				
IYOB	JOB	H347	‌	אִיּוֹב
ee-yobe'; From H340; hated (that is, persecuted); Ijob, the patriarch famous for his patience: - Job.				
IYQANYOS	ICONIUM	G2430	‌	אִיקָנְיוֹס
ee-kon'-ee-on; Perhaps from G1504; image like; Iconium, a place in Asia Minor: - Iconium.				
IYZEBEL	JEZEBEL	H348	‌	אִיזֶבֶל
'izebhel; From H336 and H2083; Baal exalts; Baal is husband to; unchaste; Izebel, the wife of king Ahab:- Jezebel				

ʾIYOB
(Job)

THE HISTORY OF ISHMAEL

Genesis 25:12 Now these are the generations of Yishma'EL, Abraham's son, whom Hagar the Mitzrim, Sarah's handmaid, bare unto Abraham:

13 And these are the names of the sons of Yishma'EL, by their names, according to their generations: the firstborn of Yishma'EL, Nebayoth; and Qedar, and Adbe'EL, and Mibsam,

14 And Mishma, and Dumah, and Massa,

15 Hadar, and Tema, Yetur (Ituraea), Naphish, and Qedemah:

16 These are the sons of Yishma'EL, and these are their names, by their towns, and by their castles; twelve princes according to their nations.

17 And these are the years of the life of Yishma'EL, an hundred and thirty and seven years: and he gave up the RUAKH and died; and was gathered unto his people.

18 And they dwelt from Khawilah unto Shur, that is before Mitzraim, as thou goest toward Asshur: and he died in the presence of all his brethren.

YISHMAEL: **ELOHIM will hear**

NEBAYOTH: **Fruitfulness**

QEDAR: **Dark Skin/Black Skin**

ADBE'EL: **Chastened of ELOHIM**

MIBSAM: **Habitation**

MISHMA: **A Report/Hearing**

DUMAH: **Silence (of Death)**

MASSA: **Burden**

KHADAR: **Chamber**

TEMA: **Desert**

YETUR: **Enclosed**

NAPHISH: **Refreshment**

QEDEMAH: **Prevented/Delayed**

THE HIDDEN PROPHECY REVEALED

Ishmael will be fruitful. He is dark skinned. ELOHIM will chasten his habitation. We hear a report of his silent burden. He will be enclosed in the chamber of the desert. His refreshment will be delayed.

Numbers 2:1 And YAHOWAH spake unto Mosheh and unto Aharon, saying,

2 Every man of the children of Yisra'EL shall pitch by his own standard, with the ensign of their father's house: far off about the tabernacle of the congregation shall they pitch.

3 And on the east side toward the rising of the sun shall they of the standard of the camp of Yehudah pitch throughout their armies: and Nakhshon the son of Amminadab shall be captain of the children of Yehudah.

4 And his host, and those that were numbered of them, were threescore and fourteen thousand and six hundred.

5 And those that do pitch next unto him shall be the tribe of Yissaskar: and Nethan'EL the son of Tzuar shall be captain of the children of Yissaskar.

6 And his host, and those that were numbered thereof, were fifty and four thousand and four hundred.

7 Then the tribe of Zebulon: and Eliab the son of Khelon shall be captain of the children of Zebulon.

8 And his host, and those that were numbered thereof, were fifty and seven thousand and four hundred.

9 All that were numbered in the camp of Yehudah were an hundred thousand and fourscore thousand and six thousand and four hundred, throughout their armies. These shall first set forth.

10 On the south side shall be the standard of the camp of Reuben according to their armies: and the captain of the children of Reuben shall be Eli'tzur the son of Shedeur.

11 And his host, and those that were numbered thereof, were forty and six thousand and five hundred.

12 And those which pitch by him shall be the tribe of Shimon: and the captain of the children of Shimon shall be Shelumi'EL the son of Tzuri-Shaddai.

13 And his host, and those that were numbered of them, were fifty and nine thousand and three hundred.

14 Then the tribe of Gad: and the captain of the sons of Gad shall be Eliasaph the son of Reu'EL.

15 And his host, and those that were numbered of them, were forty and five thousand and six hundred and fifty.

16 All that were numbered in the camp of Reuben were an hundred thousand and fifty and one thousand and four hundred and fifty, throughout their armies. And they shall set forth in the second rank.

17 Then the tabernacle of the congregation shall set forward with the camp of the Lewy'im in the midst of the camp: as they encamp, so shall they set forward, every man in his place by their standards.

18 On the west side shall be the standard of the camp of Ephrayim according to their armies: and the captain of the sons of Ephrayim shall be Elishama the son of Ammihud.

19 And his host, and those that were numbered of them, were forty thousand and five hundred.

20 And by him shall be the tribe of Manassheh: and the captain of the children of Manassheh shall be Gamli'EL the son of Pedahtzur.

21 And his host, and those that were numbered of them, were thirty and two thousand and two hundred.

22 Then the tribe of Benyamin: and the captain of the sons of Benyamin shall be Abidan the son of Gideoni.

23 And his host, and those that were numbered of them, were thirty and five thousand and four hundred.

24 All that were numbered of the camp of Ephrayim were an hundred thousand and eight thousand and an hundred, throughout their armies. And they shall go forward in the third rank.

25 The standard of the camp of Dan shall be on the north side by their armies: and the captain of the children of Dan shall be Akhiezer the son of Ammishaddai.

26 And his host, and those that were numbered of them, were threescore and two thousand and seven hundred.

27 And those that encamp by him shall be the tribe of Asher: and the captain of the children of Asher shall be Pagi'EL the son of Okran.

28 And his host, and those that were numbered of them, were forty and one thousand and five hundred.

29 Then the tribe of Naphtali: and the captain of the children of Naphtali shall be Akhira the son of Enan.

30 And his host, and those that were numbered of them, were fifty and three thousand and four hundred.

31 All they that were numbered in the camp of Dan were an hundred thousand and fifty and seven thousand and six hundred. They shall go hindmost with their standards.

32 These are those which were numbered of the children of Yisra'EL by the house of their fathers: all those that were numbered of the camps throughout their hosts were six hundred thousand and three thousand and five hundred and fifty.

33 But the Lewy'im were not numbered among the children of Yisra'EL; as YAHOWAH commanded Mosheh.

34 And the children of Yisra'EL did according to all that YAHOWAH commanded Mosheh: so they pitched by their standards, and so they set forward, every one after their families, according to the house of their fathers.

VERSE 3:

Yehudah: Praise

Nakhshon: Divine

Amminadab: My People are Noble

Yehudah is Divine, My People are Noble

VERSE 5:

Yissaskar: Reward

Nethan'EL: ELOHIM has Given

Tzuar: Brought Low

The Reward that ELOHIM has Given is Brought Low

VERSE 7:

Zebulon: Habitation

Eliab: ELOHIM is My Father

Khelon: Strong

His Habitation is with Father ELOHIM, He is Strong

VERSE 10:

Reuben: Behold a Son

Eli'tzur: ELOHIM is My Rock

Shedeur: Spread Light

Behold the Son of ELOHIM is My Rock who Spreads Light

VERSE 12:

Shimon: Hearing

Shelumi'EL: ELOHIM of My Shalom

Tzuri-Shaddai: My Rock is Mighty

The ELOHIM of My Shalom will Hear, My Rock is Mighty

VERSE 14:

Gad: Overcome

Eliasaph: My ELOHIM will Gather

Reu'EL: ELOHIM is My Friend

He will Overcome and My ELOHIM will Gather His Friends

VERSE 17:

Lewy'im: Join

and will Join

VERSE 18:

Ephrayim: Fruitful

Elishama: My ELOHIM will Hear

Ammihud: Splendor of My People

Ephrayim and My ELOHIM will Hear the People of Splendor

VERSE 20:

Manassheh: Forget

Gamli'EL: ELOHIM is My Reward

Pedahtzur: My Rock has Ransomed

They have Forgotten the Reward of ELOHM that our Rock has Ransomed

VERSE 22:

Benyamin: Son of The Right Hand

Abidan: My Father is Judge

Gideoni: Warrior

The Son of The Right Hand is the Father's Judgement and Warrior

GENEALOGY OF THE CAMPS

VERSE 25:

Dan: Judge
Akhiezer: **My Brother Helped**
Ammishaddai: **My People are Mighty**

The Judge will Help My Brother and the People of The Almighty

VERSE 27:

Asher: **Happy**
Pagi'EL: **Violence of ELOHIM**
Okran: **Trouble**

The Happy One is Troubled by the Violence of ELOHIM

VERSE 29:

Naphtali: **My Wrestling**
Akhira: **My Brother is Evil**
Enan: **Eyes**

He will Wrestle My Brother with the Evil Eye

THE HIDDEN PROPHECY REVEALED

Yehudah is Divine, My people are noble. The reward that ELOHIM has given is brought low. His habitation is with Father ELOHIM, He is strong. Behold the Son of ELOHIM is My Rock who spreads Light. The ELOHIM of My shalom will hear, My Rock is mighty.

He will overcome and My ELOHIM will gather His friends and will join Ephrayim. ELOHIM will hear the people of splendor. They have forgotten the reward of ELOHM that our Rock has ransomed. The Son of the Right Hand is the Father's Judgement and Warrior.

The Judge will help My brother and the people of The Almighty. The Happy One is troubled by the violence to ELOHIM. He will wrestle My brother with the Evil Eye

KAPH

K aph is the eleventh letter of the Hebrew alphabet. The letter Kaph symbolizes a palm or an open hand. As a suffix (Kaph-Sophit) it is used to represent: you or your. The numeric value of Kaph is 20.

K- INDEX

HEBREW/ARAMAIC PRONUNCIATION	ENGLISH TRANSLATION	STRONG'S NUMBER	ANCIENT (PALEO) HEBREW	BIBLICAL HEBREW
KALEB	CALEB	H3612	96y	כָּלֵב

kaw-labe';
dog; a form of H3611, or else from the same root in the sense of forcible; Caleb, the name of three Yisraelim (Israelites): - Caleb.

| KASDIM | CHALDEAN(S) | H3778 | ⁿⱽ△wy | כַּשְׂדִי כַּשְׂדִים |

kas-dee', kas-dee'-maw;
(Occasionally shown as the second form with enclitic; meaning towards the Kasdites); patronymic from H3777 (only in the plural); a Kasdite, or descendant of Kesed; by implication a Chaldaean (as if so descended); also an astrologer (as if proverbial of that people): - into Chaldea), patronymicallyn. from H3777 (only in the plural); a Kasdite; or descendant of Kesed; by implication a Chaldan (as if so descended); also an astrologer (as if proverbial of that people): - Chaldeans, Chaldees, inhabitants of Chaldea.

| KENA'AN | CANAAN/ PHENICE | H3667 | yoyy | כְּנַעַן |

ken-ah'-an;
From H3665; humiliated; Kenaan, a son of Ham; also the country inhabited by him: - Canaan, merchant, traffick.

| KENA'ANIM/ KENA'ANITH | CANAANITE(S) | H3669 | ⁿⱽyoyy | כְּנַעֲנִי כְּנַעֲנִים |

ken-ah'-an;
From H3665; humiliated; Kenaan, a son of Ham; also the country inhabited by him: - Canaan, merchant, traffick.

| KEPAR-NAKHUM | CAPERNAUM | G2584 | ⁿⱽAⱼ-ⱼy | כְּפַר־נַחוּם |

H.I.S. WORD

HEBREW/ARAMAIC PRONUNCIATION	ENGLISH TRANSLATION	STRONG'S NUMBER	ANCIENT (PALEO) HEBREW	BIBLICAL HEBREW
cap-er-nah-oom'; Of Hebrew origin (probably [H3723] and [H5151]); Capernaum (that is, Caphanachum), a place in Palestine: - Capernaum.				
KEPHA	PETER/CEPHAS	G2786	⨯𝙹𝖵𝗒	כֵּיפָא
kay-fah'; Of Chaldee origin (compare [H3710]); the Rock; Cephas (that is, Kepha), surname of Peter: - Cephas.				
KERAN	CHERAN	H3763	𝟿𝟦𝗒	כְּרָן
ker-awn' harp; lyre; *Keran*, an aboriginal Idumaean: - Cheran.				
KERETHIM	CHERETHITES	H3774	𝗆𝖵⨯𝟦𝗒	כְּרֵתִי כְּרֵתִים
ker-ay-thee'; Probably from H3772 in the sense of executioner; a Kerethite or life guardsman (compare H3876), (only collectively in the singular as plural): - Cherethims, Cherethites.				
KHABAQUQ	HABAKKUK	H2265	ᕈᕈᕈᕈᕑᕒ	חֲבַקּוּק
khab-ak-kook'; By reduplication from H2263; embrace; Chabakkuk, the prophet: - Habakkuk.				
KHAGGAI	HAGGAI	H2292	𝖵𝟷𝖡	חַגַּי
khag-gah'ee; From H2282; festive; Khaggai, a Hebrew prophet: - Haggai.				
KHAGITH	HAGGITH	H2294	⨯𝖵𝟷𝖡	חַגִּית

K- INDEX

HEBREW/ARAMAIC PRONUNCIATION	ENGLISH TRANSLATION	STRONG'S NUMBER	ANCIENT (PALEO) HEBREW	BIBLICAL HEBREW
khag-gheeth'; Feminine of H2291; festive; Chaggith, a wife of David: - Haggith.				
KHAM	HAM	H2526	𐤌𐤇	חָם
khawm; The same as H2525; hot (from the tropical habitat); Cham, a son of Noah; also (as a patronymic) his descendants or their country: - Ham.				
KHAMOR	HAMOR	H2544	𐤓𐤅𐤌𐤇	חֲמוֹר
kham-ore'; The same as H2543; ass; Chamor, a Canaanite: - Hamor.				
KHANAH	HANNAH	H2584	𐤄𐤍𐤇	חַנָּה
khan-naw'; From H2603; favored; Channah, an Israelitess: - Hannah.				
KHANANYAH	HANANIAH/ ANANIAS/ ANNAS	H2608	𐤄𐤉𐤍𐤍𐤇	חֲנַנְיָה
khan-an-yaw', khan-an-yaw'-hoo; From H2603 and H3050; YAH has favored; Chananyah, the name of thirteen Yisraelim (Israelites): - Hananiah.				
KHANOK	ENOCH	H2585	𐤊𐤅𐤍𐤇	חֲנוֹךְ
khan-oke'; From H2596; initiated; dedicated; educated; Chanok, an antediluvian patriarch: - Enoch.				
KHANUKKAH	HANUKKAH		𐤄𐤊𐤍𐤇	חֲנֻכָּה

HEBREW/ARAMAIC PRONUNCIATION	ENGLISH TRANSLATION	STRONG'S NUMBER	ANCIENT (PALEO) HEBREW	BIBLICAL HEBREW
a Yisraelim (Israelites) Holy Day commemorating the rededication of the Holy Temple (the Second Temple) in Jerusalem at the time of the Maccabean Revolt against the Seleucid Empire. Hanukkah is observed for eight nights and days, starting on the 25th day of Kislev according to the Hebrew calendar, which may occur at any time from late November to late December in the Gregorian calendar. It is also known as the Festival of Lights and the Feast of Dedication.				
KHATZOR	HAZOR	H2674	٩≻Xᗺ	חָצוֹר
khaw-tsore'; A collective form of H2691; village; Chatsor, the name (thus simply) of two places in Palestine and of one in Arabia: - Hazor.				
KHAWAH	EVE	H2332	ᗺ≻ᗺ	חַוָּה
khaww-waw'; Causative from H2331; lifegiver; Chavvah (or Eve), the first woman: - Eve.				
KHAZAEL	HAZAEL	H2371	6≻⪽ᗺ	חֲזָאֵל
khaz-aw-ale', khaz-aw-ale'; From H2372 and H410; Elohim has seen; Chazael, a king of Syria: - Hazael.				
KHEBRON	HEBRON	H2275	⅃٩٩9ᗺ	חֶבְרוֹן
kheb-rone'; From H2267; seat of association; Chebron, a place in Palestine, also the name of two Yisraelim (Israelites): - Hebron.				
KHEBRONIM	HEBRONITE(S)	H2276	✓⅃٩٩9ᗺ	חֶבְרוֹנִי
kheb-rone'; From H2267; seat of association; Chebron, a place in Palestine, also the name of two Yisraelim (Israelites): - Hebron.				

K- INDEX

HEBREW/ARAMAIC PRONUNCIATION	ENGLISH TRANSLATION	STRONG'S NUMBER	ANCIENT (PALEO) HEBREW	BIBLICAL HEBREW
KHELON	HELON	H2497	𐤇𐤋𐤍	חֵלֹן
khay-lone'; From H2428; *strong*; *Chelon*, an Israelite: - Helon				
KHEMDAN	HEMDAN	H2533	𐤇𐤌𐤃𐤍	חֶמְדָּן
khem-dawn' From H2531; *pleasant*; *Chemdan*, an Idumaean: - Hemdan.				
KHEPHTZI-BAH	HEPHZIBAH	H2657	𐤇𐤐𐤑𐤉-𐤁𐤄	חֶפְצִי־בָהּ
khef-tsee' baw; From H2656 with suffixes; my delight (is) in her; Cheptsibah, a fanciful name for Palestine: - Hephzi-bah.				
KHERMON	HERMON	H2768	𐤇𐤓𐤌𐤅𐤍	חֶרְמוֹן
kher-mone'; From H2763; abrupt; Chermon, a mount of Palestine: - Hermon.				
KERUB KERUBIM	CHERUB CHERUBIMS	3742	𐤊𐤓𐤅𐤁𐤉𐤌	כְּרוּב כְּרוּבִים
ker-oob'; Of uncertain derivation; a cherub or imaginary figure: - cherub, [plural] cherubims.				
KHETZRON	HEZRON	H2696	𐤇𐤑𐤓𐤅𐤍	חֶצְרוֹן
khets-rone'; From H2691; courtyard; a walled fence; Chetsron, the name of a place in Palestine; also fo two Yisraelim (Israelites): - Hezron.				
KHILQIYAHU	HILKIAH	H2518	𐤇𐤋𐤒𐤉𐤄	חִלְקִיָּה

HEBREW/ARAMAIC PRONUNCIATION	ENGLISH TRANSLATION	STRONG'S NUMBER	ANCIENT (PALEO) HEBREW	BIBLICAL HEBREW
khil-kee-yaw', khil-kee-yaw'-hoo; From H2506 and H3050; portion of YAH; Chilhiyah, the name of eight Yisraelim (Israelites): - Hilkiah.				
KHIROM/ KHIRAM	HIRAM/ IRAM	H2438	ᒿᑊᐯᓕ	חִירֹם
khee-rawm', khee-rome'; Another form of H2361; whiteness, noble; Chiram or Chirom, the name of two Tyrians: - Hiram, Huram.				
KHITTIM	HITTITES(S)	H2850	ᒿᐯ᙭ᐯᓕ	חִתִּי חִתִּים
khayth; From H2865; terror; Cheth, an aboriginal Canaanite: - Heth.				
KHIZQIYAHU	HEZEKIAH/ HIZKIAH/ HIZKIJAH/ EZEKIAS	H2396	ᓕᒿᐯᑴᙄᐯᓕ	חִזְקִיָּהוּ
khiz-kee-yaw', khiz-kee-yaw'-hoo, yekh-iz-kee-yaw', yekh-iz-kee-yaw'-hoo From H2388 and H3050; strengthened of YAH; Chizkijah, a king of Judah, also the name of two other Israelites: - Hezekiah, Hizkiah, Hizkijah. Compare H3169.				
KHOREB	HOREB	H2722	ᒿᑴᓕ	חֹרֵב
kho-rabe'; From H2717; desolate; Choreb, a (generic) name for the Sinaitic mountains: - Horeb.				
KHORI KHORIM	HORITE	H2752	ᐯᑴᓕ	חֹרִי
kho-ree' From H2356; cave dweller or troglodyte; a Chorite or aboriginal Idumaean: - Horims, Horites.				
KHULDAH	HULDAH	H2467	ᒲᐊᑰᓕ	חֻלְדָּה

K- INDEX

HEBREW/ARAMAIC PRONUNCIATION	ENGLISH TRANSLATION	STRONG'S NUMBER	ANCIENT (PALEO) HEBREW	BIBLICAL HEBREW
khool-daw'; Feminine of H2467; weasel; Chuldah, an Israelitess: - Huldah.				
KITTIM	CAPPADOCIANS/ ROMANS	H3794	⟪paleo⟫	כִּתִּי כִּתִּים
kit-tee', kit-tee-ee'; Patrial from an unused name denoting Cyprus (only in the plural); a *Kittite* or Cypriote; hence an *islander* in general, that is, the Greeks or Romans on the shores opposite Palestine: - Chittim, Kittim.				
KORAZIN	CHORAZIN	G5523	⟪paleo⟫	כּוֹרָזִין
khor-ad-zin'; Of uncertain derivation, Chorazin, a place in Palestine: - Chorazin.				
KORESH	CYRUS	H3566	⟪paleo⟫	כּוֹרֶשׁ
ko'-resh, ko'-resh; From the Persian; Koresh (or Cyrus), the Persian king: - Cyrus.				
KUSH	CUSH	H3568	⟪paleo⟫	כּוּשׁ
koosh; Probably of foreign origin; Cush (or Ethiopia), the name of a son of Ham, and of his territory; also of a Yisraeli (Israelite): - Chush, Cush, Ethiopia.				
KUSHIM	ETHIOPIANS/ CUSHITES	H3569	⟪paleo⟫	כּוּשִׁי כּוּשִׁים
koo-shee' Patronymic from H3568; a Cushite, or descendant of Cush: - Cushi, Cushite, Ethiopian (-s).				

H.I.S. WORD

LAMED

Lamed is the twelfth letter of the Hebrew alphabet. Lamed is also a Hebrew word that means to: study or learn. Symbolically Lamed represents a shepherd's staff. The numeric value is 30.

HEBREW/ARAMAIC PRONUNCIATION	ENGLISH TRANSLATION	STRONG'S NUMBER	ANCIENT (PALEO) HEBREW	BIBLICAL HEBREW
LEMEK	LAMECH	H3929	𐤉𐤌𐤋	לֶמֶךְ
leh'-mek; powerful; *Lemek*, the name of two antediluvian patriarchs: - Lamech.				
LEWI	LEVI	H3878	𐤉𐤅𐤋	לֵוִי
lay-wee'; From H3867; attached; Levi, a son of Jacob: - Levi. See also H3879, H3881				
LEWY'IM	LEVITE(S)	H3881	𐤌𐤉𐤅𐤋	לְוִיֵּי לְוִיִּם
lay-wee-ee', lay-wee'; Patronymic from H3878; a Leviite or descendant of Levi: attached - Levite.				
LIBNI	LOMNI	H3845	𐤉𐤍𐤁𐤋	לִבְנִי
lib-nee'; From H3835; *white*; *Libni*, an Israelite: - Libni.				
LOTAN	LOTAN	H3877	𐤍𐤈𐤅𐤋	לוֹטָן
lo-tawn' From H3875; *covering*, *Lotan*, an Idumaean: - Lotan.				
LUDQEYA	LAODICEA	G2993	𐤀𐤉𐤒𐤃𐤅𐤋	לוּדְקִיָא
Lah-od-ik'-i-ah; From a compound of G2992 and G1349; Laodicia, a place in Asia Minor: the people's judgement - Laodicea.				
LUQONYA	LYCAONIA	G3072	𐤀𐤉𐤍𐤒𐤅𐤋	לוּקוֹנִיָא

HEBREW/ARAMAIC PRONUNCIATION	ENGLISH TRANSLATION	STRONG'S NUMBER	ANCIENT (PALEO) HEBREW	BIBLICAL HEBREW
loo-kah-on-ee'-ah; Perhaps remotely from G3074; Lycaonia, a region of Asia Minor: wolf, (white) wolf - Lycaonia.				
LUQYA	LYCIA	G3073	ⱶⱱⱷ⧹6	לוּקְיָא
loo-kee'-ah; Probably remotely from G3074; Lycia, a province of Asia Minor: white wolf- Lycia.				
MA'AT	MAATH	H4591	⊗O𝓂	מְעַט
maw-at'; A primitive root; properly to *pare* off, that is, *lessen*; intransitively to *be* (or causatively to *make*) *small* or *few* (or figuratively *ineffective*): - suffer to decrease, diminish, (be, X borrow a, give, make) few (in number, -ness), gather least (little), be (seem) little, (X give the) less, be minished, bring to nothing.				
MADAI/ MADIM	MEDIA/MEDES	H4074	ⱱ⧍𝓂	מָדַי
maw-dah'ee; Of foreign derivation; Madai, a country of central Asia: - Madai, Medes, Media.				
MAGDAL	MAGDALA	H4026	6⧍ⱱ𝓂	מִגְדָּל
mig-dawl', mig-daw-law'; From H1431; a tower (from its size or height); by analogy a rostrum; figuratively a (pyramidal) bed of flowers: - castle, flower, pulpit, tower. Compare the names following.				
MAHALAL'EL	MAHALALEEL/ MALELEEL	H4111	6ⱶ66ⱼ𝓂	מַהֲלַלְאֵל
mah-hal-al-ale'; From H4110 and H410; *praise of ELOHIM*; *Mahalalel*, the name of an antediluvian patriarch and of an Israelite: - Mahalaleel.				

L-M INDEX

HEBREW/ARAMAIC PRONUNCIATION	ENGLISH TRANSLATION	STRONG'S NUMBER	ANCIENT (PALEO) HEBREW	BIBLICAL HEBREW
MAKABI	MACCABEE	NOT LISTED	𐤌𐤊𐤁𐤉	מַכְּבִי

The name Maccabee is often used as a synonym for the entire Hasmonean dynasty, One explanation of the name's origins is that it derives from the Aramaic "makkaba", "the hammer", in recognition of Yehudah's ferocity in battle.The traditional Yehudim explanation is that Maccabee (Hebrew: מכבים Machabi, מכבים) is an acronym for the Torah verse that was the battle-cry of the Maccabees, "Mi kamocha ba'elim YAHOWAH", "Who is like You among the Elohim"

HEBREW/ARAMAIC PRONUNCIATION	ENGLISH TRANSLATION	STRONG'S NUMBER	ANCIENT (PALEO) HEBREW	BIBLICAL HEBREW
MAKHANAIM	MAHANAIM	H4266	𐤌𐤇𐤍𐤉𐤌	מַחֲנָיִם

makh-an-ah'-yim;
Dual of H4264; double camp; Machanajim, a place in Palestine: - Mahanaim.

HEBREW/ARAMAIC PRONUNCIATION	ENGLISH TRANSLATION	STRONG'S NUMBER	ANCIENT (PALEO) HEBREW	BIBLICAL HEBREW
MAKHLI	MOOLI	H4249	𐤌𐤇𐤋𐤉	מַחְלִי

makh-lee';
From H2470; sick; Machli, the name of two Israelites: - Mahli.

HEBREW/ARAMAIC PRONUNCIATION	ENGLISH TRANSLATION	STRONG'S NUMBER	ANCIENT (PALEO) HEBREW	BIBLICAL HEBREW
MAKPELAH	MACHPELAH	H4375	𐤌𐤊𐤐𐤋𐤄	מַכְפֵּלָה

mak-pay-law';
From H3717; a fold; Makpelah, a place in Palestine: - Machpelah.

HEBREW/ARAMAIC PRONUNCIATION	ENGLISH TRANSLATION	STRONG'S NUMBER	ANCIENT (PALEO) HEBREW	BIBLICAL HEBREW
MALKITZEDEK	MELCHIZEDEK	H4442	𐤑𐤃𐤒-𐤊𐤋𐤌	מַלְכִּי–צֶדֶק

mal-kee-tseh'-dek;
From H4428 and H6664; king of right; Malki-Tsedek, an early king in Palestine: - Melchizedek.

HEBREW/ARAMAIC PRONUNCIATION	ENGLISH TRANSLATION	STRONG'S NUMBER	ANCIENT (PALEO) HEBREW	BIBLICAL HEBREW
MANA	MENAN	G3104	𐤌𐤍𐤀	מַנָּא

mah'nah
soothsayer; enchanted; Mainan, an Israelite: - Mainan.

HEBREW/ARAMAIC PRONUNCIATION	ENGLISH TRANSLATION	STRONG'S NUMBER	ANCIENT (PALEO) HEBREW	BIBLICAL HEBREW
MANAKHATH	MANAHATH	H4506	XAﬠﬠ	מְנַחַת

maw-nakh'-ath
From H5117; *rest*; *Manachath*, the name of an Edomite and of a place in Moab: - Manahath.

| MANASSHEH | MANASSEH/ MANASSES | H4519 | ﬡwﬠﬠ | מְנַשֶּׁה |

men-ash-sheh';
From H5382; causing to forget; Menashsheh, a grandson of Ya'aqob (Jacob), also the tribe descendant from him, and its territory: - Manassheh.

| MAQDON | MACEDONIA | G3110 | ﬠﬡ◁ﬓﬠ | מַקְדוֹן |

mak-ed-ohn';
Of uncertain derivation; a Macedon (Macedonian), that is, inhabitant of Macedonia: - of Macedonia, Macedonian.

| MAQQEDAH | MAKKEDAH | H4719 | ﬡ◁ﬓﬠ | מַקְדָה |

mak-kay-daw';
From the same as H5348 in the denominative sense of herding (compare H5349); fold; Makkedah, a place in Palestine: - Makkedah.

| MARQOS | MARK/ MARCUS | G3138 | ﬤﬡﬓﬡﬠ | מַרְקוֹס |

mar'-kos;
a defense; Marcus, a Christian: - Marcus, Mark.

| MATTHAN | MATTAN/ MATTHAN | H4976 | ﬠXﬠ | מַתָּן |

mat-tawn';
From H5414; a *present:* - gift, to give, reward.

HEBREW/ARAMAIC PRONUNCIATION	ENGLISH TRANSLATION	STRONG'S NUMBER	ANCIENT (PALEO) HEBREW	BIBLICAL HEBREW
MATTHAT	MATTHAT/ MATHAT	H4991	XXᵐ	מַתָּת

mat-tawth';
Feminine of H4976 abbreviated; a *present:* - gift, reward.

| MATTITYAHU | MATTHEW/ MATTATHIAS | H4993 | ૧૩⁴XXᵐ | מַתִּתְיָהוּ |

mat-tith-yaw', mat-tith-yaw'-hoo;
From H4991 and H3050; gift of YAH; Mattithyah, the name of four Yisraelim (Israelites): - Mattithiah.

| MATZOTH | FEAST OF UNLEAVENED BREAD | H4682 | ૩ᴵᵐ | מַצָּה |

matstsâh, mats-tsaw';
From H4711 in the sense of greedily devouring for sweetness; properly sweetness; concretely sweet (that is, not soured or bittered with yeast); specifically an unfermented cake or loaf, or (elliptically) the festival of Passover (because no leaven was then used): - unleavened (bread, cake), without leaven.

| MAZZAROTH | MAZZAROTH | H4216 | X૧૧ᴵᵐ | מַזָּרוֹת |

maz-zaw-raw';
Apparently from H5144 in the sense of distinction; some noted constellation (only in the plural), perhaps collectively the zodiac: - Mazzoroth. Compare H4208.

| MELEAH | MELEAH/ MELEA | H4395 | ૩⪽6ᵐ | מְלֵאָה |

mel-ay-aw';
Feminine of H4392; something *fulfilled*, that is, *abundance* (of produce): - (first of ripe) fruit, fulness.

| MELKI | MELCHI | H4428 | ⪽y6ᵐ | מֶלְכִי |

mehl'kee;
From H4427; a my *king:* - king, royal.

HEBREW/ARAMAIC PRONUNCIATION	ENGLISH TRANSLATION	STRONG'S NUMBER	ANCIENT (PALEO) HEBREW	BIBLICAL HEBREW
MEPHO'AR	EPIPHANES	NOT LISTED	𐤀𐤀𐤀𐤀	מְפוֹאָר

magnificent; **Epiphanes** (Greek:), meaning "God Manifest" or "the Glorious/Illustrious", is an ancient Greek epithet borne by several Hellenistic rulers:

| MESHIAKH (HA' MESHIAKH) | MESSIAH ANOINTED/ ANOINTED ONE | H4899 | 𐤄𐤔𐤌 | מָשִׁיחַ |

maw-shee'-akh;
From H4886; *anointed*; usually a *consecrated* person (as a king, priest, or saint); specifically the *Messiah:* - anointed, Messiah, The Anointed One.

| METUSHELAKH | METHUSELAH/ MATHUSALA | H4968 | 𐤄𐤋𐤔𐤀𐤕𐤌 | מְתוּשֶׁלַח |

meth-oo-sheh'-lakh;
his death shall send; *man of a dart; Methushelach,* an antediluvian patriarch: - Methuselah.

| MIDYAN | MIDIAN | H4079 | 𐤍𐤉𐤃𐤌 | מִדְיָן |

midyân, mid-yawn';
A variation for H4066: - brawling, contention (-ous).

| MIDYANIM | MIDIANITE(S) | H4084 | 𐤉𐤍𐤉𐤍𐤃𐤌 | מִדְיָנִי מִדְיָנִים |

mid-yaw-nee';
brawling, contention; Patronymic or patrial from H4080; a Midjanite or descendant (native) of Midjan: - Midianite. Compare H4092.

| MIGDALAH | MAGDALENE | H4026 | 𐤄𐤋𐤃𐤂𐤌 | מִגְדָּלָה |

<table>
<tr><th>HEBREW/ARAMAIC PRONUNCIATION</th><th>ENGLISH TRANSLATION</th><th>STRONG'S NUMBER</th><th>ANCIENT (PALEO) HEBREW</th><th>BIBLICAL HEBREW</th></tr>
<tr><td colspan="5">mig-dawl', mig-daw-law';
From H1431; a tower (from its size or height); by analogy a rostrum; figuratively a (pyramidal) bed of flowers: - castle, flower, pulpit, tower. Compare the names following.</td></tr>
<tr><td>MIKAEL</td><td>MICHAEL</td><td>H4317</td><td>𐤌𐤉𐤊𐤀𐤋</td><td>מִיכָאֵל</td></tr>
<tr><td colspan="5">me-kaw-ale';
From H4310 and (the prefixed derivation from) H3588 and H410; who (is) like Elohim?; Mikael, the name of an archangel and of nine Yisraelim (Israelites): - Michael.</td></tr>
<tr><td>MILKAH</td><td>MELCHA/ MILCAH</td><td>H4435</td><td>𐤌𐤋𐤊𐤄</td><td>מִלְכָּה</td></tr>
<tr><td colspan="5">mil-kaw'
A form of <u>H4436</u>; queen; Milcah, the name of a Hebrewess and of an Israelite: - Milcah.</td></tr>
<tr><td>MIRYAM</td><td>MIRIAM/ MARY</td><td>H4813</td><td>𐤌𐤓𐤉𐤌</td><td>מִרְיָם</td></tr>
<tr><td colspan="5">meer-yawm';
From H4805; rebelliously; bitterness; Mirjam, the name of two Israelitesses: - Miryam</td></tr>
<tr><td>MITZRAIM</td><td>EGYPT</td><td>H4714</td><td>𐤌𐤑𐤓𐤉𐤌</td><td>מִצְרַיִם</td></tr>
<tr><td colspan="5">mits-rah'-yim;
Dual of H4693 (distress) (limit); Mitsrajim, that is, Upper and Lower Egypt: - Egypt, Egyptians, Mizraim.</td></tr>
<tr><td>MITZRIM</td><td>EGYPTIAN(S)</td><td>H4713</td><td>𐤌𐤑𐤓𐤉𐤌</td><td>מִצְרִי
מִצְרִים</td></tr>
<tr><td colspan="5">mits-ree';
From H4714 (distress) (limit); a Mitsrite, or inhabitant of Mitsrajim: - Egyptian, of Egypt.</td></tr>
</table>

HEBREW/ARAMAIC PRONUNCIATION	ENGLISH TRANSLATION	STRONG'S NUMBER	ANCIENT (PALEO) HEBREW	BIBLICAL HEBREW
MIZZAH	MIZZAH	H4199	ꝫᏓꝫ	מִזָּה

miz-zaw'
Probably from an unused root meaning to *faint* with fear; *terror*; *Mizzah*, an Edomite: - Mizzah.

| MOABIM | MOABITE(S) | H4125 | | מוֹאָבִי מוֹאָבִים |

mo-awb;
From a prolonged form of the prepositional prefix "m-" and H1; from (her (the mother's)) father; Moab, an incestuous son of Lot; also his territory and descendants: - Moab (progenator of Chinese race).

| MOPH/ MOPHIAN | MEMPHIS | H4644 | | מֹף |

môph; *mofe;*
Of Egyptian origin; *Moph*, the capital of Lower Egypt: - Memphis. Compare H5297.

| MORDEKAI | MORDECAI | H4782 | | מָרְדֳּכַי |

mor-dek-ah'ee;
little man; Mordecai, a Yisraeli (Israelite): - Mordecai, cousin and adoptive father of queen Esther.

| MORIYAH | MORIAH | H4179 | | מוֹרִיָה |

mo-ree-yaw', mo-ree-yaw';
From H7200 and H3050; seen of YAH; Moriyah, a hill in Palestine: - Moriah.

| MOSHEH | MOSES | H4872 | | מֹשֶׁה |

HEBREW/ARAMAIC PRONUNCIATION	ENGLISH TRANSLATION	STRONG'S NUMBER	ANCIENT (PALEO) HEBREW	BIBLICAL HEBREW
mo-sheh'; From H4871; drawing out (of the water), that is, rescued; Mosheh, the Yisraelim (Israelites) lawgiver: - Moses.				
MUSHI	MOUSES	H4187	𐤇𐤅𐤔𐤌	מוּשִׁי
moo-shee', mush-shee'; From H4184; sensitive; Mushi, a Levite: - Mushi.				

ל LEWY'IM
(Levite)

א THE GENEALOGY OF YAHOSHUA

Matthew 1:1 THE book of the generation of YAHOSHUA HA' MESHIAKH, the son of Dawid, the son of Abraham.

2 Abraham begat Yitzkhaq; and Yitzkhaq begat Ya'aqob; and Ya'aqob begat **Yehudah (Judah/Judas/ Jude/Judea)** and his brethren;

3 And Yehudah begat Peretz and Zerakh of Tamar; and Peretz begat Khetzron; and Khetzron begat Aram;

4 And Aram begat Aminadab; and Aminadab begat Nakhshon; and Nakhshon begat Salmon;

5 And Salmah begat Bo'az of Rakhab; and Bo'az begat Obed of Ruth; and Obed begat Yishai;

6 And Yishai begat Dawid the king; and Dawid the king begat Shelomoh of her that had been the wife of UriYAH;

7 And Shelomoh begat Rekhabam; and Rekhabam begat AbiYAH; and AbiYAH begat Asa;

8 And Asa begat Yahoshaphat; and Yahoshaphat begat Yahoram; and Yahoram begat UzziYAH;

9 And UzziYAH begat Yotham; and Yotham begat Akhaz; and Akhaz begat KhizqiYAHU;

10 And KhizqiYAHU begat Manassheh; and Manassheh begat Amon; and Amon begat YoshiYAHU;

11 And YoshiYAHU begat YekonYAH and his brethren, about the time they were carried away to Babel:

12 And after they were brought to Babel, YekonYAH begat Shalti'EL; and Shalti'EL begat Zerubabel;

13 And Zerubabel begat Abihud; and Abihud begat El'yaqim; and El'yaqim begat Azor;

14 And Azor begat Tzadoq; and Tzadoq begat Yoqim; and Yoqim begat Elihud;

15 And Elihud begat Eleazar; and Eleazar begat Matthan; and Matthan begat Ya'aqob;

16 And Ya'aqob begat Yoseph the husband of **Miryam (Mary/Miriam)**, of whom was born YAHOSHUA, who is called MESHIAKH.

17 So all the generations from Abraham to Dawid are fourteen generations; and from Dawid until the carrying away into Babel are fourteen generations; and from the carrying away into Babel unto MESHIAKH are fourteen generations.

18 Now the birth of YAHOSHUA HA' MESHIAKH was on this wise: When as his mother Miryam was espoused to Yoseph, before they came together, she was found with child of the RUAKH HA' QODESH.

19 Then Yoseph her husband, being a just man, and not willing to make her a publick example, was minded to put her away privily.

20 But while he thought on these things, behold, the Angel of YAHOWAH appeared unto him in a dream, saying, Yoseph, thou son of Dawid, fear not to take unto thee Miryam thy wife: for that which is conceived in her is of the RUAKH HA' QODESH.

21 And she shall bring forth a son, and thou shalt call his name YAHOSHUA: for he shall save his people from their sins.

VERSE 1:	VERSE 2:
YAHOSHUA HA' MESHIAKH	Yitzkhaq: **Laughter**
Dawid: **Beloved One**	Ya'aqob: **Supplanter**
Abraham: **Father of a multitude**	Yehudah: **Praise**

YAHOSHUA HA' MESHIAKH, The Beloved One from The Father of Multitudes	Shall Laugh with Ya'aqob and Yehudah

H.I.S. WORD CONCORDANCE

VERSE 3:

Peretz: Breach

Zerakh: Rising Light

Tamar: Erect

Khetzron: Fenced Wall

Ram: Exalted

Shall Breach the Walled Fence Erected and Exalted with His Rising Light

VERSE 4:

Aminadab: My People are Liberal

Nakhshon: Divine

Salmon: Clothing

My People are Liberal with Divine Clothing

VERSE 5:

Bo'az: In Him is Strength

Rakhab: Broad

Obed: Serving

Ruth: Friend

Yishai: He Hath

His Strength is Broad, He is our Servant and Friend, He Hath

VERSE 6:

Dawid: Beloved

Shelomoh: Peaceful

UriYAH: YAH is My Light

Dawid's Peace, YAHOWAH is My Light

VERSE 7:

Rekhabam: Enlarged the People

AbiYAH: YAHOWAH is My Father

Asa: Healer

YAHOWAH My Father has Enlarged the People and Healed them.

VERSE 8:

Yahoshaphat: YAHOWAH Judged

Yahoram: YAHOWAH Raised

UzziYAH: YAHOWAH Is My Strength

YAHOWAH Judged and YAHOWAH has Raised. YAHOWAH Is My Strength

VERSE 9:

Yotham: YAHOWAH is Perfect

Akhaz: Possessor

KhizqiYAHU: Strengthened of YAHOWAH

YAHOWAH is Perfect, He is our Possessor, YAHOWAH is My Strength

VERSE 10:

Manassheh: Cause to Forget

Amon: Training

YoshiYAHU: Foundation of YAHOWAH

We have Forgotten our Training, the Foundation of YAHOWAH

VERSE 11:

YekonYAH: YAHOWAH will Establish

YAHOWAH will Establish

VERSE 12:

Shalti'EL: I Asked ELOHIM

Zerubabel: Descended of Babylon

I Asked ELOHIM for the Descendants of Babylon

VERSE 13:

Abihud: Father of Renown

El'yaqim: ELOHIM of Raising

Azor: Helpful

The Father of Renown, ELOHIM has Raised and Helped

VERSE 14:

Tzadoq: Just

Yoqim: YAHOWAH Will Raise

Elihud: ELOHIM of Majesty

The Just, YAHOWAH Will Raise the ELOHIM of Majesty

YAHOSHUA GENEALOGY IN MATTHEW

VERSE 15:

Eleazar: **ELOHIM is Helper**

Matthan: **A Gift**

Ya'aqob: **Supplanter**

ELOHIM Helped Ya'aqob with a Gift

VERSE 16:

Yoseph: **He Will Add**

Miryam (Mary/Miriam): Bitterness

YAHOSHUA MESHIAKH

YAHOSHUA MESHIAKH He Will Gather the Bitter Ones

THE HIDDEN PROPHECY REVEALED

YAHOSHUA HA' MESHIAKH, The Beloved One from The Father of Multitudes, shall laugh with Ya'aqob. Yehudah with His Rising Light shall breach the exalted fenced wall that was erected. My people are liberal with Divine clothing. He is broad in His strength. He is our Servant and Friend. He hath the shalom of Dawid, **YAHOWAH** is My Light.

YAHOWAH My Father has enlarged the people and healed them. **YAHOWAH** judged and **YAHOWAH** has raised. **YAHOWAH** Is My strength. **YAHOWAH** is perfect. He is our Possessor, **YAHOWAH** is My strength. We have forgotten our training, and foundation of **YAHOWAH**. I asked ELOHIM **YAHOWAH** to establish the descendants of Babylon. The Father of Renown, ELOHIM has raised them and helped them.

The Just One, **YAHOWAH** will rise, the ELOHIM of Majesty. ELOHIM helped Ya'aqob with a gift. **YAHOSHUA HA'MESHIAKH** He will gather the Bitter Ones.

NUN

Nun is the fourteenth letter of the Hebrew alphabet. The Nun is defined as: continuity. The symbolic representation is a seed. Nun's numerical value is 50.

N- INDEX

<table>
<tr><th>HEBREW/ARAMAIC PRONUNCIATION</th><th>ENGLISH TRANSLATION</th><th>STRONG'S NUMBER</th><th>ANCIENT (PALEO) HEBREW</th><th>BIBLICAL HEBREW</th></tr>
<tr><td>NA'AMI</td><td>NAOMI</td><td>H5281</td><td>𐤍𐤏𐤌𐤉</td><td>נָעֳמִי</td></tr>
<tr><td colspan="5">no-om-ee';
From H5278; pleasant; Noomi, an Israelitess: - Naomi.</td></tr>
<tr><td>NAKHATH</td><td>NAHATH</td><td>H5184</td><td>𐤍𐤇𐤕</td><td>נַחַת</td></tr>
<tr><td colspan="5">nakh'-ath
The same as H5183; quiet; restful; Nachath, the name of an Edomite and of two Israelites: - Nahath.</td></tr>
<tr><td>NAKHOR</td><td>NAHOR/
NACHOR</td><td>H5152</td><td>𐤍𐤇𐤅𐤓</td><td>נָחוֹר</td></tr>
<tr><td colspan="5">naw-khore';
From the same as H5170; breathe hard; snorer; Nachor, the name of the grandfather and a brother of Abraham: - Nahor.</td></tr>
<tr><td>NAKHSHON</td><td>NAASHON/
NAHSHON/
NAASSON</td><td>H5177</td><td>𐤍𐤇𐤔𐤅𐤍</td><td>נַחְשׁוֹן</td></tr>
<tr><td colspan="5">nakh-shone';
From H5172; divine; enchanter; Nachshon, an Israelite: - Naashon, Nahshon.</td></tr>
<tr><td>NAKHUM</td><td>NAHUM</td><td>H5151</td><td>𐤍𐤇𐤅𐤌</td><td>נַחוּם</td></tr>
<tr><td colspan="5">nakh-oom';
From H5162; comfortable; Nachum, a Yisraeli (Israelite) prophet: - Nahum.</td></tr>
<tr><td>NAPHTALI</td><td>NAPHTALI</td><td>H5321</td><td>𐤍𐤐𐤕𐤋𐤉</td><td>נַפְתָּלִי</td></tr>
<tr><td colspan="5">naf-taw-lee';
From H6617; my wrestling; Naphtali, a son of Jacob, with the tribe descended from him, and its territory: - Naphtali.</td></tr>
<tr><td>NAQDIMON</td><td>NICODEMUS</td><td>G3530</td><td>𐤍𐤒𐤃 𐤉𐤌𐤅𐤍</td><td>נַקְדִּימוֹן</td></tr>
</table>

HEBREW/ARAMAIC PRONUNCIATION	ENGLISH TRANSLATION	STRONG'S NUMBER	ANCIENT (PALEO) HEBREW	BIBLICAL HEBREW

nik-od'-ay-mos;
From G3534 and G1218; victorious among his people; Nicodemus, a Yisraeli (Israelite): - Nicodemus.

NARQISOS	NARCISSUS	G3488	‡ᛝᛣᛝ᚛ᛎᛄ᚛ᛎ	נַרְקִיסוֹס

nar'-kis-sos;
A flower of the same name, from nark (stupefaction, as a "narcotic"); Narcissus, a Roman: - Narcissus.

NATHAN	NATHAN	H5416	ᛎ᙭ᛎ	נָתָן

naw-thawn';
From H5414; given; Nathan, the name of five Israelites: - Nathan.

NAZARIM	NAZARITE(S)	H5139	ᛎᛝᚨᛚ᚛ᛎ	נָזִיר נְזָרִים

naw-zeer', naw-zeer';
From H5144; separate, that is, consecrated (as prince, a Nazirite); hence (figuratively from the latter) an unpruned vine (like an unshorn Nazirite). (The translation, Nazarite, is by a false alliteration with Nazareth.): - Nazarite [by a false alliteration with Nazareth], separate (-d), vine undressed.

NEBAYOTH	NEBAIOTH/ NEBAJOTH	H5032	᙭ᛝᚨᛝᛄ	נְבָיוֹת

neb-aw-yoth';
Feminine plural from H5107; fruitfulnesses; flourish; Nebajoth, a son of Ishmael, and the country settled by him: - Nebaioth, Nebajoth.

NEBUKAD'NETZAR	NEBUCHADNEZ ZAR/ NEBUCHADREZZ AR	H5019	ᛝᚱ᙭ᛝᚨ᚛ᛣᛄ᚛ᛄᛝᛄ	נְבוּכַדְנֶאצַּר

neb-oo-kad-nets-tsar', neb-oo-kad-rets-tsar', neb-oo-kad-tsore;
Of foreign derivation; Nebukadnetstsar (or retststar, or retstsor), king of Babylon: - Nebuchadnezzar, Nebuchadrezzar.

N- INDEX

<table>
<tr><th>HEBREW/ARAMAIC PRONUNCIATION</th><th>ENGLISH TRANSLATION</th><th>STRONG'S NUMBER</th><th>ANCIENT (PALEO) HEBREW</th><th>BIBLICAL HEBREW</th></tr>
<tr><td>NEKHEMYAH</td><td>NEHEMIAH</td><td>H5166</td><td>𐤍𐤇𐤌𐤉𐤄</td><td>נְחֶמְיָה</td></tr>
<tr><td colspan="5">nekh-em-yaw';
From H5162 and H3050; consolation of YAH; Nechemyah, the name of three Yisraelim (Israelites): - Nehemiah.</td></tr>
<tr><td>NEPHILIM</td><td>GIANTS/ MONSTERS</td><td>H5303</td><td>𐤍𐤐𐤉𐤋𐤉𐤌</td><td>נְפִילִים</td></tr>
<tr><td colspan="5">nef-eel', nef-eel';
From H5307; properly, a fallen one, that is, a monster or tyrant: - giant.</td></tr>
<tr><td>NERIYAH</td><td>NERIJAH/ NERIAH/ NERI</td><td>H5374</td><td>𐤍𐤓𐤉𐤄</td><td>נֵרִיָּה</td></tr>
<tr><td colspan="5">nay-ree-yaw'; nay-ree-yaw'-hoo
From H5216 and H3050; light of YAH; Nerijah, an Israelite: - Neriah.</td></tr>
<tr><td>NETHANEL</td><td>NETHANEEL/ NETHANEL</td><td>H5417</td><td>𐤍𐤕𐤍𐤀𐤋</td><td>נְתַנְאֵל</td></tr>
<tr><td colspan="5">neth-an-ale';
From H5414 and H410; given of Elohim (God); Nethanel, the name of ten Israelites: - Nethaneel.</td></tr>
<tr><td>NETHANYAH</td><td>NETHANIAH</td><td>H5418</td><td>𐤍𐤕𐤍𐤉𐤄</td><td>נְתַנְיָה</td></tr>
<tr><td colspan="5">neth-an-yaw', neth-an-yaw'-hoo;
From H5414 and H3050; given of YAH; Nethanyah, the name of four Yisraelim (Israelites): - Nethaniah.</td></tr>
<tr><td>NETZARETH</td><td>NAZARETH</td><td>G3478</td><td>𐤍𐤑𐤓𐤕</td><td>נְצָרֶת</td></tr>
<tr><td colspan="5">nad-zar-eth', nad-zar-et';
Of uncertain derivation; Nazareth or Nazaret, a place in Palestine: the guarded one - Nazareth.</td></tr>
</table>

HEBREW/ARAMAIC PRONUNCIATION	ENGLISH TRANSLATION	STRONG'S NUMBER	ANCIENT (PALEO) HEBREW	BIBLICAL HEBREW
NINWEH	NINEVEH	H5210	𐤉𐤅𐤍𐤉𐤍	נִינְוֵה

<table>
<tr><td colspan="5">nee-nev-ay';
abode of Ninus; Nineveh, the capital of Assyria: - Nineveh.</td></tr>
</table>

| NIQANOR | NICANOR | G3527 | 𐤉𐤅𐤍𐤒𐤉𐤍 | נִיקָנוֹר |

<table>
<tr><td colspan="5">nik-an'-ore;
Probably from G3528; victorious; Nikanor, a Messianic: - Nikanor.</td></tr>
</table>

| NIQOLAOS | NICOLAS | G3532 | 𐤎𐤋𐤒𐤉𐤍 | נִיקְלָס |

<table>
<tr><td colspan="5">nik-ol'-ah-os;
From G3534 and G2004; victorious over the people; Nicolaus, a heretic: - Nicolaus.</td></tr>
</table>

| NOAKH | NOAH/ NOE | H5146 | 𐤇𐤍 | נֹחַ |

<table>
<tr><td colspan="5">no'-akh;
The same as H5118; rest; Noach, the patriarch of the flood: - Noah.</td></tr>
</table>

| NOGAH | NOGAH/ NAGGE | H5051 | 𐤇𐤂𐤍 | נֹגַה |

<table>
<tr><td colspan="5">no'-gah;
From H5050; brilliancy (literally or figuratively): - bright (-ness), light, (clear) shining.</td></tr>
</table>

(OH) WAW

Waw is the sixth letter of the Hebrew tongue. It is also the 3rd letter in the Names of YAHOWAH (יהוה) and YAHOSHUA (יהושע). As a prefix Waw means: and (the conjunction). As a suffix Waw means: his. The symbolic meaning is that of a nail or a hook. Waw can take on 3 different pronunciations: U (ooo), O (oh) and W. The numeric value is 6.

HEBREW/ARAMAIC PRONUNCIATION	ENGLISH TRANSLATION	STRONG'S NUMBER	ANCIENT (PALEO) HEBREW	BIBLICAL HEBREW
paw-ras'; Of foreign origin; *Paras* (that is, *Persia*), an Eastern country, including its inhabitants: - Persia, Persians.				
PARGEMOS	PERGAMOS	G4010	𐤐𐤓𐤂𐤌𐤅𐤎	פַּרְגְּמוֹס
per'-gam-os; From G4444; fortified; Pergamus, a place in Asia Minor: - Pergamos.				
PARUSH	PHARISEE	G5330	𐤐𐤓𐤅𐤔	פָּרוּשׁ
Pharisaios, far-is-ah'-yos; Of Hebrew origin (compare [H6567]); to *separate*, literally (to *disperse*) or figuratively (to *specify*); also (by implication) to *wound:* - scatter, declare, distinctly, shew, sting.; a separatist, that is, exclusively religious; a Pharisaean, that is, Jewish sectary: - Pharisee.				
PAWLOS	PAUL	G3972	𐤐𐤅𐤋𐤅𐤎	פּוֹלוֹס
pow'-los; Of Latin origin; (little; but remotely from a derivative of G3973, meaning the same); Paulus, the name of a Roman and of an apostle: - Paul, Paulus.				
PEDAHTZUR	PEDAHZUR	H6301	𐤐𐤃𐤄𐤑𐤅𐤓	פְּדָהצוּר
ped-aw-tsoor'; From H6299 and H6697; a *rock* (that is, Elohim (God)) *has ransomed*; *Pedahtsur*, an Israelite: - Pedahzur.				
PELATHIM	PELETHITES	H6432	𐤐𐤋𐤕𐤉𐤌	פְּלֵתִי פְּלֵתִים
pel-ay-thee'; From the same form as H6431; a courier (collectively) or official messenger: - Pelethites.				

O-P INDEX

HEBREW/ARAMAIC PRONUNCIATION	ENGLISH TRANSLATION	STRONG'S NUMBER	ANCIENT (PALEO) HEBREW	BIBLICAL HEBREW
OBADYAH	OBADIAH	H5662	𐤄𐤉𐤃𐤏𐤏	עֹבַדְיָה
o-bad-yaw', o-bad-yaw'-hoo; Active participle of H5647 and H3050; serving YAH; Obadyah, the name of thirteen Yisraelim (Israelites): - Obadiah.			
OBED	OBED	H5744	𐤃𐤏𐤏	עֹבֵד
o-bade'; Active participle of H5647; serving; Obed, the name of five Israelites: - Obed.			
OKRAN	OCRAN	H5918	𐤍𐤓𐤊𐤏	עָכְרָן
ok-rawn'; From H5916; muddler; Okran, an Israelite: - Ocran.			
OMAR	OMAR	H201	𐤓𐤌𐤀	אוֹמָר
o-mawr' From H559; talkative; Omar, a grandson of Esau: - Omar.			
ONAM	ONAM	H208	𐤌𐤍𐤀	אוֹנָם
o-nawm' A variation of H209; strong; Onam, the name of an Edomite and of an Israelite: - Onam.			
PAGIEL	PAGIEL	H6295	𐤋𐤀𐤉𐤏𐤂𐤐	פַּגְעִיאֵל
pag-ee-ale'; From H6294 and H410; accident of Elohim (God); Pagiel, an Israelite: - Pagiel.			
PARAS/ PARSIM	PERSIA/ PERSIANS	H6539	𐤎𐤓𐤐	פָּרַס פָּרְסִים

H.I.S. WORD

HEBREW/ARAMAIC PRONUNCIATION	ENGLISH TRANSLATION	STRONG'S NUMBER	ANCIENT (PALEO) HEBREW	BIBLICAL HEBREW
PELEG	PELEG/ PHALEC	H6389	7ﬠﬖ	פֶּלֶג

peh'-leg;
river, stream, division; earthquake; The same as H6388; *earthquake*; *Peleg*, a son of Shem: - Peleg.

| PERATH | EUPHRATES | H6578 | X٩ﬖ | פְּרָת |

per-awth';
From an unused root meaning to break forth; rushing; Perath (that is, Euphrates), a river of the East: - Euphrates.

| PERETZ | PEREZ/ PHAREZ/ PHARES | H6556 | ﬧﬠﬖ | פֶּרֶץ |

peh'-rets;
From H6555; a *break* (literally or figuratively): - breach, breaking forth (in), X forth, gap.

| PERIZZIM | PERIZZITE(S) | H6522 | ﬠﬖ | פְּרִזִּי |

per-iz-zee';
For H6521; inhabitant of the open country; a Perizzite, one of the Canaanitish tribes: - Perizzite.

| PERUSHIM | PHARISEES | G5330 | ﬠﬖ | פְּרוּשִׁים |

Pharisaios, far-is-ah'-yos;
Of Hebrew origin (compare [H6567]); A primitive root; to *separate*, literally (to *disperse*) or figuratively (to *specify*); also (by implication) to *wound*: - scatter, declare, distinctly, shew, sting; a separatist, that is, exclusively religious; a Pharisaean, that is, Jewish sectary: - Pharisee.

| PESAKH | PASSOVER | H6453 | ﬨﬤﬖ | פֶּסַח |

HEBREW/ARAMAIC PRONUNCIATION	ENGLISH TRANSLATION	STRONG'S NUMBER	ANCIENT (PALEO) HEBREW	BIBLICAL HEBREW
peh'-sakh; From H6452; a pretermission, that is, exemption; used only technically of the Jewish Passover (the festival or the victim): - passover (offering).				
PHAR'OH	PHARAOH	H6547	𐤖𐤏𐤓𐤐	פַּרְעֹה
par-o'; Of Egyptian derivation; Paroh, taxing the dead; a generic title of Egyptian kings: - Pharaoh.				
PHELISHTIM	PHILISTINE(S)	H6430	𐤌𐤉𐤕𐤔𐤋𐤐	פְּלִשְׁתִּי פְּלִשְׁתִּים
pel-eh'-sheth; From H6428; rolling, that is, migratory; Pelesheth, a region of Syria: - Palestina, Palestine, Philistia, Philistines.				
PHILADELPHIYA	PHILADELPHIA	G5359	𐤀𐤉𐤐𐤋𐤃𐤋𐤉𐤐	פִילָדֶלְפִיָא
Philadelphos (the same as G5361), a king of Pergamos; Philadelphia, a place in Asia Minor: brotherly love - Philadelphia.				
PHILIPOS	PHILIP	G5376	𐤎𐤀𐤉𐤋𐤉𐤐	פִּילִפּוֹס
fil'-ip-pos; From G5384 and G2462; fond of horses; Philippus, the name of four Yisraelim (Israelites): - Philip.				
PHUBI	PHEBE	G5402	𐤉𐤁𐤅𐤐	פוּבִי
foy'-bay; Feminine of Phoibos (bright; probably akin to the base of G5457); Phaebe, a Messianic woman: - Phebe.				

HEBREW/ARAMAIC PRONUNCIATION	ENGLISH TRANSLATION	STRONG'S NUMBER	ANCIENT (PALEO) HEBREW	BIBLICAL HEBREW
PILATOS	PILATE	G4091	‡ꚍ⊗Ꮣᐯꓓ	פִּילָטוֹס

<table>
<tr><td colspan="5">pil-at'-os;
Of Latin origin; close pressed, that is, firm; Pilatus, a Roman: - Pilate.</td></tr>
</table>

| PINKHAS | PHINEHAS | H6372 | ‡ᖴꓓᎩᐯꓓ | פִּינְחָס |

<table>
<tr><td colspan="5">pee-nekh-aws';
Apparently from H6310 and a variation of H5175; mouth of a serpent; Pinechas, the name of three Yisraelim (Israelites): - Phinehas.</td></tr>
</table>

| PINOQYA | PHENICE | G5403 | ⋉ᐯꟼᎩᐯꓓ | פִּינוּקְיָא |

<table>
<tr><td colspan="5">foy-nee'-kay;
From G5404; palm country; Phaenice (or Phaenicia), a region of Palestine: - Phenice, Phenicia.</td></tr>
</table>

| PORQIOS | PORCIUS | G4201 | ‡ꚍᐯꟼꓬꓓ | פָּרְקִיוֹס |

<table>
<tr><td colspan="5">por'-kee-os;
Of Latin origin; apparently swinish; Porcius, a Roman: - Porcius.</td></tr>
</table>

| POTIPHAR | POTIPHAR | H6318 | ꓫꓓꓯ⊗ꚍꓓ | פּוֹטִיפַר |

<table>
<tr><td colspan="5">pôtyphar; po-tee-far';
belonging to the sun; Potiphar, an Egyptian: - Potiphar.</td></tr>
</table>

| PRISQELAH | PRISCILLA | G4252 | ᏩᏴꟼ‡ᐯꓓ | פְּרִיסְקְלָה |

<table>
<tr><td colspan="5">pris'-cil-lah;
Diminutive of G4251; ancient; Priscilla (that is, little Prisca), a Messianic woman: - Priscilla.</td></tr>
</table>

| PURIM | PURIM | H6332 | ꮇᐯꓬꓓ | פּוּרִים |

O-P INDEX

HEBREW/ARAMAIC PRONUNCIATION	ENGLISH TRANSLATION	STRONG'S NUMBER	ANCIENT (PALEO) HEBREW	BIBLICAL HEBREW
poo-reem' From H6331; a lot (as by means of a broken piece): - Pur, Purim.				
PUT	LIBYA	H6316	⊗לﬧ	פוּט
poot; a bow; Put, a son of Ham, also the name of his descendants or thier region, and of a Persian tribe: Libya - Phut, Put.				

QOPH

Q oph is the nineteenth letter of the Hebrew tongue. Qoph symbolically represents the back of the head. The numerical value of Qoph is 100.

HEBREW/ARAMAIC PRONUNCIATION	ENGLISH TRANSLATION	STRONG'S NUMBER	ANCIENT (PALEO) HEBREW	BIBLICAL HEBREW
QAHATHIM	KOHATHITE(S)	H6956	ᵞⱽ✗ᴲᗊ	קְהָתִי קְהָתִים

keh-hawth';
From an unused root meaning to ally oneself; allied; Kehath, a Yisraeli (Israelite): - Kohath.

| QANAH | CANA | H7071 | ᴲᎩᗊ | קָנָה |

kaw-naw';
Feminine of H7070; reediness; Kanah, the name of a stream and of a place in Palestine: - Kanah.

| QANDAQ | CANDACE | G2582 | ᗊᐃᎩᗊ | קַנְדְּק |

kan-dak'-ay;
prince of servants; Candace, an Egyptian queen: - Candace.

| QAPOD'QIYAH | CAPPADOCIA | G2587 | ᴲⱽᗊᐃᎩᗊ | קַפּוֹדְקִיָּה |

kap-pad-ok-ee'-ah;
province of good horses; Cappadocia, a region of Asia Minor: - Cappadocia.

| QAYAPHA | CAIAPHAS | G2533 | ᐊᎩⱽᗊ | קַיָּפָא |

kah-ee-af'-as;
as comely; the dell; Caiaphas (that is, Cajepha), a Yisraeli (Israelite): - Caiaphas.

| QAYIN | CAIN | H7030 | Ꭹⱽᗊ | קַיִן |

qayin; kah'-yin;
From H6969 in the original sense of fixity; a lance (as striking fast): - spear.

| QAYNAN | CAINAN | H7018 | ᎩᎩⱽᗊ | קֵינָן |

HEBREW/ARAMAIC PRONUNCIATION	ENGLISH TRANSLATION	STRONG'S NUMBER	ANCIENT (PALEO) HEBREW	BIBLICAL HEBREW
kay-nawn'; possession; *Kenan*, an antediluvian: - Cainan, Kenan.				
QEASAR	CAESAR	G2541	٩≠∀٩	קֵיסָר
Kah'ee-sar; Of Latin origin; Caesar, a title of the Roman emperor: - Csar.				
QEHATH	KOHATH	H6955	×٦٩	קְהָת
keh-hawth'; From an unused root meaning to ally oneself; allied; Kehath, a Yisraeli (Israelite): - Kohath.				
QELODAH	CLAUDA	G2802	٦◿ל٦٩	קְלֹודָה
klow'-day; Of uncertain derivation; Claude, an island near Crete: - Clauda.				
QELOPHAH	CLEOPHAS	G2832	≠﹁ל٦٩	קְלֹופָס
klo-pas'; Of Chaldee origin (corresponding to G256); Clopas, a Yisraeli (Israelite): - Clopas.				
QENAZ	KENAZ	H7073	⅄﹁٩	קְנַז
ken-az' Probably from an unused root meaning to *hunt*; hunter; *Kenaz*, the name of an Edomite and of two Israelites: - Kenaz.				
QERETI	CRETE	G2914	∀⊗∀٦٩	קְרֵיטִי
kray'-tay; Of uncertain derivation; Crete, an island in the Mediterranean: - Crete.				

HEBREW/ARAMAIC PRONUNCIATION	ENGLISH TRANSLATION	STRONG'S NUMBER	ANCIENT (PALEO) HEBREW	BIBLICAL HEBREW
QERISIQIM	CRESCENS	G2913	ⵊⵖ ⵕⵝⴶⵖⵕⵖ	קְרִיסְקִים

krace'-kace;
Of Latin origin; growing; Cresces (that is, Crescens), a Messianic: - Crescens.

| QERISPOS | CRISPUS | G2921 | ⵊⵕⵕⴶⵖⴽ | קְרִיסְפּוֹס |

kris'-pos;
Of Latin origin; "crisp"; Crispus, a Corinthian: - Crispus.

| QESARIYAH | CAESAREA | G2542 | ⵕⵖⵕⵕⴶⵖⵕ | קֵיסַרְיָה |

kahee-sar'-i-a;
From G2541; Caesaria, the name of two places in Palestine: - Csarea.

| QETURAH | KETURAH | H6989 | ⵕⵕⵕⵡⵕⵕ | קְטוּרָה |

ket-oo-raw';
Feminine passive participle of H6999; perfumed; Keturah, a wife of Abraham: - Keturah.

| QIDRON | CEDRON | H6939 | ⵊⵕⵕⴸⵕⵕ | קִדְרוֹן |

kid-rone';
From H6937; dusky place; Kidron, a brook near Jerusalem: - Kidron.

| QILEMES | CLEMENT | G2815 | ⵕⵖⵊⵖ ⵊⵕ | קְלִימִיס |

klay'-mace;
Of Latin origin; merciful; Clemes (that is, Clemens), a Messianic: - Clement.

| QILIQYA | CILICIA | G2791 | ⴽⵖⵕⵖⵍⵖⵕ | קִילִיקְיָא |

kil-ik-ee'-ah;
the land of Celix; Cilicia, a region of Asia Minor: - Cilicia.

HEBREW/ARAMAIC PRONUNCIATION	ENGLISH TRANSLATION	STRONG'S NUMBER	ANCIENT (PALEO) HEBREW	BIBLICAL HEBREW
QIPHROS	CYPRUS	G2954	⧫᠀᠀ᘚ᠀ᘔ	קִיפְרוֹס

koo'-pros;
Of uncertain origin; Cyprus, an island in the Mediterranean: - Cyprus.

| QIRENIOS | CYRENIUS | G2958 | ⧫᠀᠀ᘔ᠀᠀᠀ᘔ | קוּרִינִיּוֹס |

koo-ray'-nee-os;
Of Latin origin; Cyrenius (that is, Quirinus), a Roman: - Cyrenius.

| QISH | KISH | H7027 | w᠀ᘔ | קִישׁ |

keesh;
From H6983; a bow; Kish, the name of five Yisraelim (Israelites): - Kish.

| QLODIOS | CLAUDIUS | G2804 | ⧫᠀᠀ᘔᘔᘔᘔ | קְלוֹדִיוֹס |

klow'-dee-os;
lame; Claudius, the name of two Romans: - Claudius.

| QODESH | HOLY | H6944 | wᘔᘔ | קֹדֶשׁ |

qôdesh, ko'-desh;
From H6942; a sacred place or thing; rarely abstractly sanctity: - consecrated (thing), dedicated (thing), hallowed (thing), holiness, (X most) holy (X day, portion, thing), saint, sanctuary.

| QORAKH | KORAH/ CORE | H7141 | ᗷ᠀ᘔ | קֹרַח |

qôrach, ko'-rakh;
From H7139; ice; Korach, the name of two Edomites and three Israelites: - Korah.

| QORINTHOS | CORINTH | G2882 | ⧫᠀᠀᠀᠀ᘔ | קוֹרִנְתוֹס |

HEBREW/ARAMAIC PRONUNCIATION	ENGLISH TRANSLATION	STRONG'S NUMBER	ANCIENT (PALEO) HEBREW	BIBLICAL HEBREW
kor'-in-thos; satiated; Corinthus, a city of Greece: - Corinth.				
QOSAM	QESEM/ COSAM	H7081	ﬡﬤﬡ	קֶסֶם
keh'-sem; From H7080; a *lot*; also *divination* (including its *fee*), *oracle:* - (reward of) divination, divine sentence, witchcraft.				
QURINI	CYRENE	G2957	ﬡﬡﬡﬡﬡ	קוּרִינִי
koo-ray'-nay; Of uncertain derivation; Cyrene, a region of Africa: - Cyrene.				

RESH

Resh is the twentieth letter in the Hebrew language. Defined as a word, Resh means: head, first or top. The numeric value is 200.

HEBREW/ARAMAIC PRONUNCIATION	ENGLISH TRANSLATION	STRONG'S NUMBER	ANCIENT (PALEO) HEBREW	BIBLICAL HEBREW
RAKHAB	RAHAB	H7343	9Β٩	רְחָב
raw-khawb';				

raw-khawb';
The same as H7342; proud; broad; wide; Rachab, a Canaanitess: - Rahab.

| RAKHEL | RACHEL | H7353 | ٤Β٩ | רְחֵל |

raw-khale';
From an unused root meaning to journey; a ewe (the females being the predominant element of a flock), (as a good traveller): - ewe, sheep.

| REKHABAM | REHOBOAM | H7346 | ꓳ09Β٩ | רְחַבְעָם |

rekh-ab-awm';
From H7337 and H5971; a people has enlarged; Rechabam, a Yisraeli (Israelite) king: - Rehoboam.

| RAM | ARAM/ RAM | H7410 | ꓳ٩ | רָם |

rawm;
Active participle of H7311; high; exalted; Ram, the name of an Arabian and of an Israelite: - Ram. See also H1027

| RENEWED MONTH | NEW MOON | H2320 | wΔΒ | חֹדֶשׁ |

kho'-desh;
From H2318; the new month; by implication a month: - month (-ly), new moon (mistranslated as "new moon")

| REPHAYAH | REPHAJAH/ REPHAIAH/ RHESA | H7509 | ꓱⱱ٦٩ | רְפָיָה |

ref-aw-yaw';
From H7495 and H3050; YAH has cured; Rephajah, the name of five Israelites: - Rephaiah.

HEBREW/ARAMAIC PRONUNCIATION	ENGLISH TRANSLATION	STRONG'S NUMBER	ANCIENT (PALEO) HEBREW	BIBLICAL HEBREW
REU	REU/ RAGAU	H7466	৭০৭	רְעוּ

reh-oo';
For H7471 in the sense of H7453; *friend*; *Reu*, a postdiluvian patriarch: - Reu.

| REUBEN | REUBEN | H7205 | ৭৯৭ | רְאוּבֵן |

reh-oo-bane';
From the imperative of H7200 and H1121; *see* ye a *son*; *Reuben*, a son of Jacob: - Reuben.

| REUBENIM | REUBENITE(S) | H7206 | ৭৯৭ | רְאוּבֵנִי רְאוּבֵנִים |

reh-oo-bay-nee';
Patronymic from H7205; a Reubenite or descendant of Reuben: behold a son-children of Reuben, Reubenites.

| REUEL | REUEL/ RAGUEL | H7467 | ৬৭৭০৭ | רְעוּאֵל |

reh-oo-ale';
From the same as H7466 and H410; *friend of Elohim (God)*; *Reuel*, the name of Moses' father in law, also of an Edomite and an Israelite: - Raguel, Reuel.

| RIBQAH | REBEKAH | H7259 | ৭৭৭৭ | רִבְקָה |

rib-kaw';
From an unused root probably meaning to clog by tying up the fetlock; fettering (by beauty); Ribkah, the wife of Isaac: - Rebekah.

| RUAKH | SPIRIT | H7307 | ৮৭৭ | רוּחַ |

HEBREW/ARAMAIC PRONUNCIATION	ENGLISH TRANSLATION	STRONG'S NUMBER	ANCIENT (PALEO) HEBREW	BIBLICAL HEBREW
rûach, roo'-akh; From H7306; wind; by resemblance breath, that is, a sensible (or even violent) exhalation; figuratively life, anger, unsubstantiality; by extension a region of the sky; by resemblance spirit, but only of a rational being (including its expression and functions): - air, anger, blast, breath, X cool, courage, mind, X quarter, X side, spirit ([-ual]), tempest, X vain, ([whirl-]) wind (-y).				
RUKHOTH	SPIRITS	H7307	XB۹٩	רוּחֹת
rûach, roo'-akh; From H7306; (plural) wind; by resemblance breath, that is, a sensible (or even violent) exhalation; figuratively life, anger, unsubstantiality; by extension a region of the sky; by resemblance spirit, but only of a rational being (including its expression and functions): - air, anger, blast, breath, X cool, courage, mind, X quarter, X side, spirit ([-ual]), tempest, X vain, ([whirl-]) wind (-y).				
RUPHOS	RUFUS	G4504	₮۹۾٩٩	רוּפוֹס
hroo'-fos; Of Latin origin; red; Rufus, a Messianic: - Rufus.				
RUTH	RUTH	H7327	X۹٩	רוּת
rooth; Probably for H7468; friend; mate; Ruth, a Moabitess: - Ruth.				

ROMI
(Rome)

ב THE GENEALOGY OF YAHOSHUA

Luke 3:23 And YAHOSHUA himself began to be about thirty years of age, being (as was supposed) the son of Yoseph, which was the son of Heli,

24 Which was the son of Matthat, which was the son of Lewi, which was the son of Melki, which was the son of Yanah, which was the son of Yoseph,

25 Which was the son of MattitYAHU, which was the son of Amotz, which was the son of Nakhum, which was the son of El-Yahoenai, which was the son of Nogah,

26 Which was the son of Ma'at, which was the son of MattitYAHU, which was the son of Shemi, which was the son of Yoseph, which was the son of Yehudah,

27 Which was the son of Yokhanan, which was the son of RephaYAH, which was the son of Zerubabel, which was the son of Shealti'EL, which was the son of NeriYAH,

28 Which was the son of Melki, which was the son of Addi, which was the son of Qosam, which was the son of Almodad, which was the son of Er,

29 Which was the son of YESHUA, which was the son of Eliezer, which was the son of Yoram, which was the son of Matthat, which was the son of Lewi,

30 Which was the son of Shimon, which was the son of Yehudah, which was the son of Yoseph, which was the son of Yonah, which was the son of El'yaqim,

31 Which was the son of Malah, which was the son of Mana, which was the son of Matathah, which was the son of Nathan, which was the son of Dawid,

32 Which was the son of Yishai, which was the son of Obed, which was the son of Bo'az, which was the son of Salmah, which was the son of Nakhshon,

33 Which was the son of Aminadab, which was the son of Aram, which was the son of Khetzron, which was the son of Peretz, which was the son of Yehudah,

34 Which was the son of Ya'aqob, which was the son of Yitzkhaq, which was the son of Abraham, which was the son of Terakh, which was the son of Nakhor,

35 Which was the son of Serug, which was the son of Reu, which was the son of Peleg, which was the son of Kheber, which was the son of Shelakh,

36 Which was the son of Qaynan, which was the son of Arpakshad, which was the son of Shem, which was the son of Noakh, which was the son of Lemek,

37 Which was the son of Metushelakh, which was the son of Khanok, which was the son of Yered, which was the son of Mahalal'EL, which was the son of Qaynan,

38 Which was the son of Enosh, which was the son of Sheth, which was the son of Adam, which was the son of ELOHIM.

VERSE 23:
YAHOSHUA

Yoseph: He Will Increase

Eli: Lofty

YAHOSHUA will Increase, He is Lofty

VERSE 24:
Matthat: Gift

Lewi: Joined

Melki: My King

Yanah: Suppress

Yoseph: He Will Add

A Gift Joined by My King was Suppressed, but He shall Add

VERSE 25:
MattitYAHU: Gift of YAH

Amotz: Strong

Nakhum: Comfortable

El-Yahoenai: My Eyes are for YAHOWAH

Nogah: Brightness

A Gift of YAH, Strong and Comfortable, My Eyes are for YAHOWAH'S Brightness

VERSE 26:
Ma'at: Small

MattitYAHU: Gift of YAH

Shemi: Famous

Yoseph: He Will Add

Yehudah: Praise

A Small Gift of YAH that is Famous, He shall Increase in Praise

VERSE 27:
Yokhanan: **YAHOWAH** Favored
RephaYAH: **YAH has Healed**
Zerubabel: **Descendants of Babylon**
Shealti'EL: **I Asked ELOHIM**
NeriYAH: **Lamp of YAH**

YAHOWAH Favored and YAH has Healed the Descendants of Babylon, I asked ELOHIM, YAH is My Lamp

VERSE 28:
Melki: **My King**
Addi: **Ornament**
Qosam: **Divine**
Almodad: **Not Measured**
Er: **Watchful**

My King's Divine Ornament Cannot be Measured, be Watchful

VERSE 29:
YESHUA: **He Will Save**
Eliezer: **My ELOHIM is Help**
Yoram: **YAHOWAH** Raised
Matthat: **Gift**
Lewi: **Joined**

YESHUA ELOHIM is My Help, **YAHOWAH** Raised Him, His Gift is Joined

VERSE 30:
Shimon: **Obedient**
Yehudah: **Praise**
Yoseph: **He Will Add**
Yonah: **Dove**
El'yaqim: **ELOHIM of Raising**

He Hears Yehudah and Yoseph, He Shall Add a DOVE, ELOHIM He shall Raise Up

VERSE 31:
Meleah: **Abundance**
Mana: **Enchanted**
Matathah: **Gift**

Nathan: **Given**
Dawid: **Beloved**

An Abundant, Enchanted Gift was Given unto Dawid

VERSE 32:
Yishai: **He Hath**
Obed: **Serving**
Bo'az: **In Him is Strength**
Salmon: **Clothing**
Nakhshon: **Divine**

He Hath a Servant, In Him is Strength, His Clothing is Divine

VERSE 33:
Aminadab: **My People are Noble**
Ram: **Exalted**
Khetzron: **Fenced Wall**
Peretz: **Breach**
Yehudah: **Praise**

My People are Noble and Exalted, The Fenced Wall Yehudah has Breached

VERSE 34:
Ya'aqob: **Supplanter**
Yitzkhaq: **Laughter**
Abraham: **Father of a multitude**
Terakh: **Delay**
Nakhor: **Breathe Hard**

Ya'aqob shall Laugh with Abraham, we Breathe Hard at His Delay

VERSE 35:
Serug: **Branch**
Reu: **Friend**
Peleg: **Stream**
Eber: **Cross Over**
Shelakh: **Sent Out**

The Branch is our Friend, He Crossed Over the Stream, He Sent Out

YAHOSHUA GENEALOGY IN LUKE

VERSE 36:
Qaynan: **Possession**
Arpakshad: **Mouth Gathers from the Breast**
Shem: **Name**
Noakh: **Comfort**
Lemek: **Powerful**

A Possession for those whose Mouth Gathers from the Breast, The COMFORTER'S Name is Powerful

VERSE 37:
Metushelakh: **His Death shall Send**
Khanok: **Dedicated**

Yered: **Descend**
Mahalal'EL: **Praise of ELOHIM**
Qaynan: **Possession**

His Death shall Send the Dedicated One to Descend, Praise ELOHIM He has Possessed

VERSE 38:
Enosh: **Mortal**
Sheth: **Substituted**
Adam: **Mankind**

Mortal Man as a Substitute for Adam.

THE HIDDEN PROPHECY REVEALED

YAHOSHUA will increase. A lofty gift is joined by my King. It was suppressed, but He shall add a gift of YAH. Strong and Comforting, My syes are for YAHOWAH'S brightness. A small gift of YAHOWAH that is famous, He shall increase in praise.

YAHOWAH favored and I asked ELOHIM. YAHOWAH has healed the descendants of Babylon. YAHOWAH is My lamp. My King's divine ornament cannot be measured. He is watchful, YESHUA ELOHIM is My help.

YAHOWAH raised Him up. His gift is joined to the obedient from Yehudah and Yoseph. He shall add The DOVE (RUAKH HA QODESH). ELOHIM, He shall raise up. An abundant, enchanted gift was given unto Dawid. He hath a Servant, in Him is strength. His clothing is Divine.

My people are noble and exalted. Yehudah has breached the fenced wall. Ya'aqob shall laugh with Abraham. We breathe hard because of His delay. The Branch is our Friend, He crossed over the stream. He is our Apostle. A possession for those whose mouth gathers from the breast.

The COMFORTER'S Name is powerful! His death shall send the Dedicated One to descend. Praise ELOHIM! He has possessed mortal man as a substitute for Adam.

SHEEN

Sheen is the 21st letter of the Hebrew language. Sheen can also be pro-
nouced as "Seen" when a small dot is positioned at the top left side of the
letter. Sheen symbolizes: eating, or destroying. Sheen is also the Hebrew word
for: teeth. Sheen is also the 4th letter in the Name YAHOSHUA (יהושע). The
numeric value is 300.

HEBREW/ARAMAIC PRONUNCIATION	ENGLISH TRANSLATION	STRONG'S NUMBER	ANCIENT (PALEO) HEBREW	BIBLICAL HEBREW
SALMAN/ SALMAH	SALMAN	H8012	𐤉𐤓𐤌𐤋𐤅	שַׁלְמוֹן

sal-mone';
From H8008; *clothing; investiture*; *Salmon*, an Israelite: - Salmon.

| SEDOM | SODOM | H5467 | 𐤌𐤃𐤎 | סְדֹם |

sed-ome';
From an unused root meaning to scorch; burnt (that is, volcanic or bituminous) district; Sedom, a place near the Dead Sea: - Sodom.

| SEIR | SEIR | H8165 | 𐤓𐤉𐤏𐤎 | שֵׂעִיר |

saw-eer', saw-eer';
From H8175; shaggy; as noun, a he goat; by analogy a faun: - devil, goat, hairy, kid, rough, satyr.

| SERUG | SERUG/ SARUCH | H8286 | 𐤂𐤅𐤓𐤎 | שְׂרוּג |

ser-oog';
From H8276; *branch*; *Serug*, a postdiluvian patriarch: - Serug.

| SHABBAT | SABBATH | H7673 | 𐤕𐤁𐤅 | שַׁבָּת |

shâbath, shaw-bath';
A primitive root; to repose, that is, desist from exertion; used in many implied relations (causatively, figuratively or specifically): - (cause to, let, make to) cease, celebrate, cause (make) to fail, keep (sabbath), suffer to be lacking, leave, put away (down), (make to) rest, rid, still, take away.

| SHALOM | PEACE | H7965 | 𐤌𐤅𐤋𐤅 | שָׁלוֹם |

HEBREW/ARAMAIC PRONUNCIATION	ENGLISH TRANSLATION	STRONG'S NUMBER	ANCIENT (PALEO) HEBREW	BIBLICAL HEBREW
shaw-lome', shaw-lome'; From H7999; *safe*, that is, (figuratively) *well, happy, friendly*; also (abstractly) *welfare*, that is, health, prosperity, peace: - X do, familiar, X fare, favour, + friend, X greet, (good) health, (X perfect, such as be at) peace (-able, -ably), prosper (-ity, -ous), rest, safe (-ly), salute, welfare, (X all is, be) well, X wholly.				
SHALTIEL	SHALTIEL/ SHEALTIEL/ SALATHIEL	H7597	6≮1×6w	שְׁלְתִּיאֵל
sheh-al-tee-ale', shal-tee-ale'; From H7592 and H410; *I have asked ELOHIM; Shealtiel*, an Israelite: - Shalthiel, Shealtiel.				
SHAMMAH	SHAMMAH	H8047	ヲりw	שַׁמָּה
sham-maw' From H8074; *ruin*; by implication *consternation*: - astonishment, desolate (-ion), waste, wonderful thing.				
SHA'UL	SAUL/ SHAUL	H7586	61≮w	שָׁאוּל
shaw-ool'; Passive participle of H7592; asked; Shaul, the name of an Edomite and two Yisraelim (Israelites): - Saul, Shaul.				
SHEBUOTH	FEAST OF WEEKS	H7620	×09w	שָׁבֻעֹת
shaw-boo'-ah, shaw-boo'-ah, sheb-oo-aw' Properly passive participle of H7650 as a denominative of H7651; literally *sevened*, that is, a week (specifically of years): - seven, week.				
SHEDEUR	SHEDEUR	H7707	11≮1△w	שְׁדֵיאוּר
shed-ay-oor'; From the same as H7704 and H217; *spreader of light; Shedejur*, an Israelite: - Shedeur.				

HEBREW/ARAMAIC PRONUNCIATION	ENGLISH TRANSLATION	STRONG'S NUMBER	ANCIENT (PALEO) HEBREW	BIBLICAL HEBREW
SHEKEM	SHECHEM	H7927	ッyw	שְׁכֶם

shek-em';
The same as H7926; ridge; Shekem, a place in Palestine: - Shechem.

| SHELAKH | SHELAH/ SALA | H7974 | ㅂ6w | שֶׁלַח |

sheh'-lakh; send out, apostle, a shoot; branch;
From H7971; a *missile* of attack, that is, *spear*; also (figuratively) a *shoot* of growth, that is, *branch:* - dart, plant, X put off, sword, weapon.

| SHELOMITH | SALOME | H7965 | XYッ ᴋ6w | שְׁלוֹמִית |

shaw-lome', shaw-lome';
From H7999; safe, that is, (figuratively) well, happy, friendly; also (abstractly) welfare, that is, health, prosperity, peace: -   X do, familiar, X fare, favour, + friend, X greet, (good) health, (X perfect, such as be at) peace (-able, -ably), prosper (-ity, -ous), rest, safe (-ly), salute, welfare, (X all is, be) well, X wholly.

| SHELOMOH | SOLOMON | H8010 | ꝫッ6w | שְׁלֹמֹה |

shel-o-mo';
From H7965; peaceful; Shelomoh, David's successor: - Solomon.

| SHELUMIEL | SHELUMIEL | H8010 | 6X̄Yッ6w | שְׁלֻמִיאֵל |

shel-oo-mee-ale';
From H7965 and H410; *peace of Elohim (God)*; *Shelumiel,* an Israelite: - Shelumiel.

| SHEM | SHEM | H8035 | ッw | שֵׁם |

shame;
name; authority; Shem, a son of Noah (original name of Melkitzedek the High Priest): - Sem, Shem.

HEBREW/ARAMAIC PRONUNCIATION	ENGLISH TRANSLATION	STRONG'S NUMBER	ANCIENT (PALEO) HEBREW	BIBLICAL HEBREW
SHEMAYAH	SHEMAIAH	H8098	ﾖﾊﾔﾘﾜ	שְׁמַעְיָה

shem-aw-yaw', shem-aw-yaw'-hoo;
From H8085 and H3050; YAH has heard; Shemayah, the name of twenty five Yisraelim (Israelites): - Shemaiah.

HEBREW/ARAMAIC PRONUNCIATION	ENGLISH TRANSLATION	STRONG'S NUMBER	ANCIENT (PALEO) HEBREW	BIBLICAL HEBREW
SHEMI	SHIMEI/ SHIMI/ SEMEI	H8096	ﾖﾘﾜ	שִׁמְעִי

shim-ee';
From H8088; famous; Shimi, the name of twenty Israelites: - Shimeah [from the margin], Shimei, Shimhi, Shimi.

HEBREW/ARAMAIC PRONUNCIATION	ENGLISH TRANSLATION	STRONG'S NUMBER	ANCIENT (PALEO) HEBREW	BIBLICAL HEBREW
SHEMUEL	SAMUEL	H8050	ﾋﾐﾘﾜ	שְׁמוּאֵל

shem-oo-ale';
From the passive participle of H8085 and H410; heard of Elohim; Shemuel, the name of three Yisraelim (Israelites): - Samuel, Shemuel.

HEBREW/ARAMAIC PRONUNCIATION	ENGLISH TRANSLATION	STRONG'S NUMBER	ANCIENT (PALEO) HEBREW	BIBLICAL HEBREW
SHEOL	HELL/ HEDES	H7585	ﾋﾊﾜ	שְׁאוֹל

sheh-ole', sheh-ole';
From H7592; hades or the world of the dead (as if a subterranian retreat), including its accessories and inmates: - grave, hell, pit.

HEBREW/ARAMAIC PRONUNCIATION	ENGLISH TRANSLATION	STRONG'S NUMBER	ANCIENT (PALEO) HEBREW	BIBLICAL HEBREW
SHEPHO	SHEPHO/ SHEPHI	H8195	ﾋﾘﾜ	שְׁפוֹ

shef-o', shef-ee'
From H8192; baldness (compare H8205); Shepho or Shephi, an Idumaean: - Shephi, Shepho.

HEBREW/ARAMAIC PRONUNCIATION	ENGLISH TRANSLATION	STRONG'S NUMBER	ANCIENT (PALEO) HEBREW	BIBLICAL HEBREW
SHETH	SETH	H8352	Xw	שֵׁת

shayth
H7896; put, that is, substituted; Sheth, third son of Adam: - Seth, Sheth.

HEBREW/ARAMAIC PRONUNCIATION	ENGLISH TRANSLATION	STRONG'S NUMBER	ANCIENT (PALEO) HEBREW	BIBLICAL HEBREW
SHILOAKH	SILOAH/ SILOAM	H7975	ᕁᏓw	שָׁלֹחַ

shee-lo'-akh, sheh'-lakh;
The second form is in imitation of H7974, used in Neh 3:15; from H7971; rill;
Shiloach, a fountain of Jerusalem: send out, appoint, spread - Shiloah, Siloah.

| SHILOH | SHILOH | H7886 | ᏃᏓᎩw | שִׁילֹה |

shee-lo';
From H7951; tranquil; Shiloh, an epithet of the Messiah: - Shiloh.

| SHIMEE | SEMEI | H8096 | ᏉᎧᎩw | שִׁמְעִי |

shim-ee';
From H8088; famous; Shimi, the name of twenty Israelites: - Shimeah [from the margin], Shimei, Shimhi, Shimi.

| SHIMON | SIMEON | H8095 | ᏃᏉᎧᎩw | שִׁמְעוֹן |

shim-one';
From H8085; hearing; obedient Shimon, one of Jacob's sons, also the tribe descendant from him: - Simeon.

| SHIMONIM | SIMEONITE(S) | H8099 | ᏃᏉᎧᎩw | שִׁמְעֹנִי שִׁמְעֹנִים |

shim-o-nee';
Patronymic from H8095; a Shimonite (collectively) or descendant of Shimon: hearing - tribe of Simeon, Simeonites.

| SHIMSHON | SAMSON | H8123 | ᏃᏆwᎩw | שִׁמְשׁוֹן |

shim-shone';
From H8121; sunlight; Shimshon, a Yisraeli (Israelite): - Samson.

HEBREW/ARAMAIC PRONUNCIATION	ENGLISH TRANSLATION	STRONG'S NUMBER	ANCIENT (PALEO) HEBREW	BIBLICAL HEBREW
SHOBAL	SHOBAL	H7732	6997w	שׁוֹבָל

sho-bawl'
From the same as H7640; *overflowing*; *Shobal*, the name of an Edomite and two Israelites: - Shobal.

| SHOMRON | SAMARIA | H8111 | 7997w | שֹׁמְרוֹן |

sho-mer-one';
From the active participle of H8104; watch station; Shomeron, a place in Palestine: - Samaria.

| SHOSHANNAH | SUSANNA | H7799 | 37w9w | שׁוֹשַׁנָּה |

sho-shan-naw';
From H7797; a lily (from its whiteness), as a flower or architectural ornament; also a (straight) trumpet (from the tubular shape): - lily, Shoshannim.

| SHUA/ BEN SHUA | SHUA/ SHUAH/ BARSABA | H7770 | O9w | שׁוּעַ |

shûa;
shoo'-ah; From H7768; a *halloo:* - cry, riches

| SIKHON | SIHON | H5511 | 79B4‡ | סִיחוֹן |

see-khone', see-khone';
From the same as H5477; tempestuous; Sichon, an Amoritish king: - Sihon.

| SILA | SILAS | G4609 | ≮6∀‡ | סִילָא |

see'-las;
woody; Contraction for G4610; Silas, a Messianic: - Silas.

| SISRA | SISERA | H5516 | ≮9‡∀‡ | סִיסְרָא |

HEBREW/ARAMAIC PRONUNCIATION	ENGLISH TRANSLATION	STRONG'S NUMBER	ANCIENT (PALEO) HEBREW	BIBLICAL HEBREW
battle array; Sisera, the name of a Canaanitish king and of one of the Nethinim: - Sisera				
SQAYWAH	SCEVA	G4630	ﬧﬦﭏﬦ	סְקָוֶה
skyoo-as'; Apparently of Latin origin; left handed; Scevas (that is, Scaevus), a Yisraeli (Israelite): - Sceva.				
STEPHANOS	STEPHEN	G4735	ﬦﬡ﬙ﬠﬦ	סְטְפָנוֹס
stef'-an-os; From an apparently primary "stepho" (to twine or wreathe); a chaplet (as a badge of royalty, a prize in the public games or a symbol of honor generally; but more conspicuous and elaborate than the simple fillet, G1238), literally or figuratively: - crown.				
SUKKOTH	FEAST OF TABERNACLES	H5521	﬩ﬡﬠﬦ	סֻכּוֹת
sûkkâh, sook-kaw'; Feminine of H5520; a hut or lair: - booth, cottage, covert, pavilion, tabernacle, tent.				

TAW

Taw is the twenty second and final letter of the Hebrew language. Defined as a letter, Taw means: mark. Symbolically Taw represents the Cross and the Last. As a prefix Taw is used to indicate 2nd person masculine and 3rd person feminine when placed in front of a verb. The numeric value is 400.

HEBREW/ARAMAIC PRONUNCIATION	ENGLISH TRANSLATION	STRONG'S NUMBER	ANCIENT (PALEO) HEBREW	BIBLICAL HEBREW
TALMAY	PTOLOMY/ PTOLEMEE	H8526	ⱽ𝗒6×	תַּלְמַי

talmay, tal-mah'ee;
From H8525; ridged; Talmai, the name of a Canaanite and a Syrian: - Talmai.

| TAMAR | TAMAR | H8558 | ⱽ𝗒× | תָּמָר |

tâmâr, taw-mawr';
From an unused root meaning to be erect; a palm tree: - palm (tree).

| TAPPUAKH | TAPPUAH | H8599 | ㅂⱽ𝖩× | תַּפּוּחַ |

tap-poo'-akh;
The same as H8598; Tappuach, the name of two places in Palestine, also of an Israelite: - Tappuah.

| TARSI | TARSUS | G5018 | ⱽ≢𝖩⊗ | טַרְסִי |

tar-syoos';
From G5019; a Tarsean, that is, native of Tarsus: a flat basket - of Tarsus.

| TEBERYAH | TIBERIAS | G5085 | ㅋⱽ𝖩ⱽ⊗ | טִיבֶרְיָה |

tib-er-ee-as';
From G5086; Tiberias, the name of a town and a lake in Palestine: - Tiberias.

| TEMAN | TEMAN | H8487 | 𝗒𝗒× | תֵּמָן |

tay-mawn'
The same as H8486; Teman, the name of two Edomites, and of the region and descendants of one of them: - south, Teman.

| TERAKH | TERAH | H8646 | ㅂⱽ× | תֶּרַח |

H.I.S. WORD CONCORDANCE

HEBREW/ARAMAIC PRONUNCIATION	ENGLISH TRANSLATION	STRONG'S NUMBER	ANCIENT (PALEO) HEBREW	BIBLICAL HEBREW
teh'-rakh; delay; station; Terach, the father of Abraham; also a place in the Desert: - Tarah, Terah.				
THIATIRA	THYATIRA	G2363	⟨paleo⟩	תִּיאֲטִירָא
thoo-at'-i-rah; Of uncertain derivation; Thyatira, a place in Asia Minor: - Thyatira.				
THO'MA	THOMAS	G2381	⟨paleo⟩	תּוֹמָא
tho-mas'; Of Chaldee origin (compare [H8380]); the twin; Thomas, a Messianic: - Thomas.				
TIBARYOS	TIBERIUS	G5086	⟨paleo⟩	טִיבֶרִיוֹס
tib-er'-ee-os; Of Latin origin; probably pertaining to the river Tiberis or Tiber; Tiberius, a Roman emperor: - Tiberius.				
TIMAI	TIMAEUS	H2931	⟨paleo⟩	טָמֵא
taw-may'; From H2930; foul in a religious sense: - defiled, + infamous, polluted (-tion), unclean.				
TIMNA	TIMNA	H8555	⟨paleo⟩	טִמְנָע
tim-naw' From H4513; restraint; Timna, the name of two Edomites: - Timna, Timnah.				
TIMOTHEOS	TIMOTHEUS/ TIMOTHY	G5095	⟨paleo⟩	טִימוֹתִיּוֹס
tee-moth'-eh-os; From G5092 and G2316; dear to Elohim; Timotheus, a Messianic: - Timotheus, Timothy.				

T- INDEX

HEBREW/ARAMAIC PRONUNCIATION	ENGLISH TRANSLATION	STRONG'S NUMBER	ANCIENT (PALEO) HEBREW	BIBLICAL HEBREW
TIRTZAH	TIRZAH	H8656	𐤄𐤑𐤓𐤕	תִּרְצָה
eer-tsaw'; From H7521; delightsomeness; Tirtsah, a place in Palestine; also an Israelitess: - also an Israelitess: - Tirzah.				
TITOS	TITUS	G5103	𐤎𐤅𐤈𐤉𐤈	טִיטוֹס
tee'-tos; Of Latin origin, nurse; Titus, a Messianic: - Titus.				
TOBIYAH	TOBIAH/ TOBIT	H2900	𐤄𐤉𐤁𐤅𐤈	טוֹבִיָה
to-bee-yaw', to-bee-yaw'-hoo; From H2896 and H3050; goodness of YAHOWAH; Tobiyah, the name of three Yisraelim and of one Samaritan: - Tobiah, Tobiyah.				
TORAH	LAW/ LAWS	H8451	𐤄𐤓𐤅𐤕	תּוֹרָה
to-raw', to-raw'; From H3384; a precept or statute, especially the Decalogue or Pentateuch: - law.				
TZADOQ	ZADOK	H6659	𐤒𐤅𐤃𐤑	צָדוֹק
tsaw-doke'; From H6663; just; Tsadok, the name of eight or nine Yisraelim: - Zadok.				
TZADUQIM	SADDUCEES	H6659	𐤌𐤉𐤒𐤅𐤃𐤑	צָדוּקִים
Probably from G4524; a Sadducaean (that is, Tsadokian), H6659 plural; or follower of a certain heretical Yisraelim: - Sadducee.				
TZEDEQYAH	ZEDEKIAH	H6667	𐤄𐤉𐤒𐤃𐤑	צִדְקִיָה

HEBREW/ARAMAIC PRONUNCIATION	ENGLISH TRANSLATION	STRONG'S NUMBER	ANCIENT (PALEO) HEBREW	BIBLICAL HEBREW
tsid-kee-yaw', tsid-kee-yaw'-hoo; From H6664 and H3050; right of YAH; Tsidkiyah, the name of six Yisraelim: - Zedekiah, Zidkiyah.				
TZELAPHKHAD	ZELOPHEHAD	H6765	𐤑𐤋𐤐𐤇𐤃	צְלָפְחָד
tsel-of-khawd'; From the same as H6764 and H259; Tselophchad, a Yisraeli: - Zelophehad.				
TZEPHO	ZEPHO	H6825	𐤑𐤐𐤅	צְפוֹ
tsef-ee' From H6822; *observant*; *Tsepho* or *Tsephi*, an Idumaean: - Zephi, Zepho.				
TZERUYAH	ZERUAH	H6871	𐤑𐤓𐤅𐤏𐤄	צְרוּעָה
tser-oo-aw'; Feminine passive participle of H6879; leprous; Tseruah, an Israelitess: - Zeruah.				
TZIBIYAH	TABITHA/ DORCAS	H6646	𐤑𐤁𐤉𐤄	צִבְיָה
tseb-ee-yaw'; Feminine of H6643; a female gazelle				
TZIBON	ZIBEON	H6649	𐤑𐤁𐤏𐤅𐤍	צִבְעוֹן
tsib-one'; From the same as H6648; *variegated*; to *dip* (into coloring fluid); a *dye:Tsibon*, an Idumaean: - Zibeon.				
TZIDON	ZIDON	H6721	𐤑𐤉𐤃𐤅𐤍	צִידוֹן
tsee-done', tsee-done'; From H6679 in the sense of catching fish; fishery; Tsidon, the name of a son of Canaan, and of a place in Palestine: - Sidon, Zidon.				

T- INDEX

HEBREW/ARAMAIC PRONUNCIATION	ENGLISH TRANSLATION	STRONG'S NUMBER	ANCIENT (PALEO) HEBREW	BIBLICAL HEBREW
TZION	ZION	H6725	ยฯฯ	צִיּוֹן

tsee-yoon';
From the same as H6723 in the sense of conspicuousness (compare H5329); a monumental or guiding pillar: - sign, title, waymark.

| TZOR | TYRE | H6865 | ฯฯ | צוֹר |

tsore, tsore;
The same as H6864; a rock; Tsor, a place in Palestine: - Tyre, Tyrus.

| TZUAR | ZUAR | H6686 | ฯๆฯ | צוּעָר |

tsoo-awr';
From H6819; small; brought low; Tsuar, an Israelite: - Zuar.

| TZURI-SHADDAI | ZURISHADDAI | H6701 | ฯๆฯ | צוּרִישַׁדָּי |

tsoo-ree-shad-dah'ee;
From H6697 and H7706; rock of (the) Almighty; Tsurishaddai, an Israelite: - Zurishaddai.

YOD

Yod is the tenth letter of the Hebrew alphabet. It is the first letter in the Names of YAH (יה), YAHOWAH (יהוה) and YAHOSHUA (יהושע). Yod is defined as: hand. As a prefix, Yod indicates the 3rd person masculine when placed in front of a verb. As a suffix, Yod indicates possessive nouns. The numeric value is 10.

HEBREW/ARAMAIC PRONUNCIATION	ENGLISH TRANSLATION	STRONG'S NUMBER	ANCIENT (PALEO) HEBREW	BIBLICAL HEBREW
URIYAH	URIAH/ URIJAH	H223	𐤉𐤅𐤓𐤅𐤀	אוּרִיָּה

oo-ree-yaw', oo-ree-yaw'-hoo;
From H217 and H3050; flame of YAH; Uriyah, the name of one Hittite and five Yisraelim (Israelites): - Uriah, Uriyah.

| UTZ | UZ | | 𐤑𐤅𐤏 | עוּץ |

oots
Apparently from H5779; *consultation*; *Uts*, a son of Aram, also a Seirite, and the regions settled by them: - Uz.

| UZZIEL | OZEEL | H5816 | 𐤋𐤀𐤉𐤅𐤏 | עֻזִּיאֵל |

ooz-zee-ale';
From H5797 and H410; *strength of ELOHIM*; *Uzziel*, the name of six Israelites: - Uzziel.

| UZZIYAH | UZZIAH | H5818 | 𐤉𐤅𐤉𐤏 | עֲזִיָּה |

ooz-zee-yaw', ooz-zee-yaw'-hoo;
From H5797 and H3050; strength of YAHOWAH; Uzziyah, the name of five Yisraelim (Israelites): - Uzziah.

| WASHTI | VASHTI | H2060 | 𐤉𐤅𐤉𐤏 | וַשְׁתִּי |

wash-tee';
Of Persian origin; *Vashti*, the queen of Xerxes: - Washti.

| WOPHSI | VOPHSI | H2058 | 𐤉𐤎𐤐𐤅 | וָפְסִי |

wof-see';
Probably from H3254; additional; Vophsi, a Yisraeli (Israelite): - Wophsi.

YAAQOB	JACOB	H3290	gᵠoɤ	יַעֲקֹב

yah-ak-obe';
From H6117; *heel catcher* (that is, supplanter); *Jaakob*, the Israelitish patriarch: - Jacob.

YABBOQ	JABBOK	H2999	ᵠgɤ	יַבֹּק

yab-boke';
Probably from H1238; pouring forth; Jabbok, a river East of the Jordan: - Jabbok.

YAHOAKHAZ	JEHOAHAZ	H3059	ƖBᐑⱯᎧᎠᏉ	יְהוֹאָחָז

yeh-ho-aw-khawz';
From H3068 and H270; YAHOWAH seized; Jehoachaz, the name of three Yisraelim (Israelites): - Jehoahaz. Compare H3099.

YAHOASH	JEHOASH	H3060	wᐑᎧᎠᏉ	יְהוֹאָשׁ

yeh-ho-awsh';
From H3068 and (perhaps) H784; YAHOWAH fired; Jehoash, the name of two Yisraelim (Israelites) kings: - Jehoash Compare H3101.

YAHOKHANAN	JEHOHANAN	H3076	ᎠᎠBᎧᎠᏉ	יְהוֹחָנָן

yeh-ho-khaw-nawn';
From H3068 and H2603; YAHOWAH-favored; Jehochanan, the name of eight Yisraelim (Israelites): - Jehohanan, Johanan. Compare H3110.

YAHONATHAN	JONATHAN		ᎠXᎠᎧᎠᏉ	יְהוֹנָתָן

yah-ho-naw-thawn'
From H3068 and H5414; YAHOWAH-given; Jehonathan, the name of four Yisraelim (Israelites): - Jonathan. Compare H3129.

YAHORAM	JEHORAM/ JORAM	H3088	ᎧᎠᎠᏉ	יְהוֹרָם

yeh-ho-rawm';
From H3068 and H7311; YAHOWAH-raised; Jehoram, the name of a Syrian and of three Yisraelim (Israelites): - Jehoram, Joram. Compare H3141.

YAHOSHAPHAT	JEHOSHAPHAT	H3092	⊗𝑗𝑤𝟃𝟥𝒱	יְהוֹשָׁפָט

yeh-ho-shaw-fawt';
From H3068 and H8199; YAHOWAH-judged; Jehoshaphat, the name of six Yisraelim (Israelites); also of a valley near Jerusalem : - Jehoshaphat. Compare H3146.

YAHOSHUA	YAHOSHUA/ YASHUA/ JOSHUA	H3091	O𝟃𝑤𝟃𝟥𝒱 O𝑤𝟃𝟥𝒱	יְהוֹשׁוּעַ יְהוֹשֻׁעַ

yah-ho-shoo'-ah;
From H3068 and H3467; YAHOWAH -saved; YAHOWAH is salvation; Jehoshua (that is, Joshua), the Yisraelim (Israelites) Messiah and only begotton Son of YAHOWAH: - Jehoshua, Jehoshuah, Joshua. Compare H1954, H3442.

YAHOWAH	YAHOWAH/ YHWH	H3068	𝟃𝟥𝟃𝒱	יְהוָה

yah-ho-waw';
From H1961; (the) self Existent or eternal; YAHOWAH (HE WAS, HE IS, HE WILL BE), Biblical Hebrew name of Elohim: - YHWH, the LORD. Compare H3050, H3069.

YAHOYADA	JEHOIADA	H3077	O∆𝒱𝟃𝟥𝒱	יְהוֹיָדָע

yeh-ho-yaw-daw';
From H3068 and H3045; YAHOWAH-known; Jehoiada, the name of three Yisraelim (Israelites): - Jehoiada. Compare H3111.

YAHOYAQIM	JEHOIAKIM	H3079	𝑚𝒱𝑞𝒱𝟃𝟥𝒱	יְהוֹיָקִים

yeh-ho-yaw-keem';
From H3068 abbreviated and H6965; YAHOWAH will raise; Jehojakim, a Yehudim king: - Jehoiakim. Compare H3113.

| YAHU | JEHU | H3058 | ᴚᵞᴚᵞ | יֵהוּא |

yay-hoo';
From H3068 and H1931; YAHOWAH (is) He; Jehu, the name of five Yisraelim (Israelites): - Jehu.

| YAIR | JAIRUS | H2971 | ᵞᵞᴚᵞ | יָאִיר |

yaw-ere';
From H215; enlightener; Jair, the name of four Yisraelim (Israelites): - Jair.

| YALAM | JAALAM/ JALAM | H3281 | ᵞᶜᴑᵞ | יַעְלָם |

yah-lawm'
From H5956; occult; Jalam, an Edomite: - Jalam.

| YAMBRIS | JAMBRES | G2387 | ᵞᵞᴚᵞᵞᵞ | יַמְבְרִיס |

ee-am-brace';
Of Egyptian origin; Jambres, an Egyptian: - Jambres.

| YANAH | JANNA | H3238 | ᵞᵞᵞ | יָנָה |

yaw-naw';
A primitive root; to rage or be violent; by implication to suppress, to maltreat: - destroy, (thrust out by) oppress (-ing, -ion, -or), proud, vex, do violence.

| YANIS | JANNES | G2389 | ᵞᵞᵞᵞ | יַנִּיס |

ee-an-nace';
Of Egyptian origin; Jannes, an Egyptian: - Jannes.

| YAPHETH | JAPHETH | H3315 | ᵡᵞᵞ | יֶפֶת |

yeh'-feth;
From H6601; expansion; Jepheth, a son of Noah; also his posterity: - Japheth.

YAPHO	JOPPA	H3305	שׁ JY	יָפוֹ

yaw-fo', yaw-fo';
From H3302; beautiful; Japho, a place in Palestine: - Japha, Joppa.

YARABAM	JEROBOAM	H3379	מֹ09שׁ Y	יָרָבְעָם

yaw-rob-awm';
From H7378 and H5971; (the) people will contend; Jarobam, the name of two
Yisraelim (Israelites) kings: - Jeroboam.

YARDEN	JORDAN	H3383	יΔשׁY	יַרְדֵּן

yar-dane';
From H3381; a descender; Jarden, the principal river of Palestine: - Jordan.

YASON	JASON	G2394	יΧ干Y	יָסוֹן

ee-as'-oan;
Future active participle masculine of G2390; about to cure; Jason, a Messianic: -
Jason.

YAWAN	GREECE	H3120	יΧY	יָוָן

yaw-vawn';
Probably from the same as H3196; effervescing (that is, hot and active); Javan, the
name of a son of Joktan, and of the race (Ionians, that is, Greeks) descended from
him, with their territory; also of a place in Arabia: - Javan.

YEBUSIM	JEBUSITE(S)	H2983	מΧ干שׁY	יְבוּסִי יְבוּסִים

yeb-oo-see';
trodden; Patrial from H2982; a Jebusite or inhabitant of Jebus: - Jebusite(-s).

YEHUDAH	JUDAH/ JUDAS/ JUDE/ JUDEA	H3063	₹Δשׁ₹Y	יְהוּדָה

yeh-hoo-daw';
From H3034; praise; celebrated; Jehudah (or Judah), literally to *use* (that is, hold out) *the hand*; physically to *throw* (a stone, an arrow) at or away; especially to *revere* or *worship* (with extended hands); intensively to *bemoan* (by wringing the hands): - cast (out), (make) confess (-ion), praise, shoot, (give) thank (-ful, -s, -sgiving).; also of the tribe descended from the first, and of its territory: - Judah.

YEHUDI/YEHUDIM	JUDAH/ JEWS/ JUDEA	H3064	𐤉𐤄𐤅𐤃𐤉	יְהוּדִי יְהוּדִים

yeh-hoo-dee';
Patronymic from H3063; a Jehudite (that is, Judaite or Jew), or descendant of Jehudah (that is, Judah): celebrated, he will praise - Jew.

YEKHEZQEL	EZEKIEL	H3168	𐤋𐤀𐤒𐤆𐤇𐤉	יְחֶזְקֵאל

yekh-ez-kale';
From H2388 and H410; Elohim will strengthen; Jechezkel, the name of two Yisraelim (Israelites): - Ezekiel, Jehezekel.

YEKONYAH	JECONIAH/ JECHONIAS	H3204	𐤄𐤉𐤍𐤊𐤉	יְכָנְיָה

yek-on-yaw'(-hoo), yek-o-neh-yaw'
From H3559 and H3050; *YAH will establish*; *Jekonjah*, a Jewish king: - Jeconiah. Compare H3659.

YERED	JARED	H3382	𐤃𐤓𐤉	יֶרֶד

yeh'-red;
From H3381; a *descent*; *Jered*, the name of an antediluvian, and of an Israelite: - Jared.

YERIKHO	JERICHO	H3405	𐤅𐤇𐤉𐤓𐤉	יְרִיחוֹ

yer-ee-kho', yer-ay-kho', yer-ee-kho';
Perhaps from H3394; his moon; or else from H7306; fragrant; Jericho or Jerecho, a place in Palestine: - Jericho.

YERUSHALEM	JERUSALEM	H3389	𐤌𐤋𐤔𐤅𐤓𐤉	יְרוּשָׁלַ͏ִם

yer-oo-shaw-lah'-im, yer-oo-shaw-lah'-yim;
A dual (in allusion to its two main hills (the true pointing, at least of the former reading, seems to be that of H3390)); probably from (the passive participle of) H3384 and H7999; founded peaceful; Jerushalaim or Jerushalem, the capital city of Palestine: - Jerusalem.

YESHAYAHU	ISAIAH	H3470	𐤅𐤄𐤉𐤏𐤔𐤉	יְשַׁעְיָהוּ

yesh-ah-yaw', yesh-ah-yaw'-hoo;
From H3467 and H3050; YAH has saved; Jeshayah, the name of seven Yisraelim (Israelites): - Isaiah, Jesaiah, Jeshaiah.

YESHUA	JESHUA	H3442	𐤏𐤅𐤔𐤉	יֵשׁוּעַ

yah-shoo'-ah;
For H3091; He will save; Jeshua, contracted name of YAHOSHUA; the name of two Yisraelim (Israelites), also of a place in Palestine: - Jeshua.

YETUR	ITURAEA	H3195	𐤓𐤅𐤈𐤉	יְטוּר

yet-oor';
Probably from the same as H2905; encircled (that is, inclosed); Jetur, a son of Ishmael: - Jetur.

YEUSH	JEUSH/ JEHUSH	H3266	𐤔𐤅𐤏𐤉	יְעוּשׁ

yeh-oosh'
From H5789; *hasty*; *Jeush*, the name of an Edomite and of four Israelites: - Jehush, Jeush. Compare H3274.

YIKHEZ'QIYAH	HEZEKIAH	H2396	𐤄𐤉𐤒𐤆𐤇𐤉	יְחִזְקִיָּה

khiz-kee-yaw', khiz-kee-yaw'-hoo, yekh-iz-kee-yaw', yekh-iz-kee-yaw'-hoo; From H2388 and H3050; strengthened of YAH; Chizkiyah, a king of Judah, also the name of two other Yisraelim (Israelites): - Hezekiah, Hizkiah, Hizkiyah. Compare H3169.				
YIPHTAKH	JEPHTHAH	H3316	𐤉𐤐𐤕𐤇	יִפְתָּח
yif-tawkh'; From H6605; he will open; Jiphtach, a Yisraeli (Israelite); also a place in Palestine: - Jephthah, Jiphtah.				
YIRMEYAHU	JEREMIAH/ JEREMY	H3414	𐤉𐤓𐤌𐤉𐤄𐤅	יִרְמְיָהוּ
yir-meh-yaw', yir-meh-yaw'-hoo; From H7311 and H3050; YAH will rise; Jirmeyah, the name of eight or nine Yisraelim (Israelites): - Jeremiah.				
YISHAI	JESSE	H3448	𐤉𐤔𐤉	יִשַׁי
yee-shah'ee, ee-shah'ee; I possess; From the same as H3426; extant; Jishai, David's father: - Jesse.				
YISHMAEL	ISHMAEL	H3458	𐤉𐤔𐤌𐤏𐤀𐤋	יִשְׁמָעֵאל
yish-maw-ale'; From H8085 and H410; Elohim will hear; Jishmael, the name of Abraham's oldest son, and of five Yisraelim (Israelites): - Ishmael.				
YISHMAELIM	ISHMAELITE(S)	H3459	𐤉𐤔𐤌𐤏𐤀𐤋𐤉𐤌	יִשְׁמָעֵאלִי יִשְׁמָעֵאלִים
yish-maw-ay-lee'; Patronymic from H3458; a Jishmaelite or descendant of Jishmael: Elohim will hear - Ishmaelite.				
YISRAEL	ISRAEL	H3478	𐤉𐤔𐤓𐤀𐤋	יִשְׂרָאֵל

yis-raw-ale'; From H8280 and H410; he will rule as Elohim; Jisrael, a symbolical name of Jacob; also (typically) of his posterity: - Israel.				
YISSASKAR	ISSACHAR	H3485	ישׂשׂכר	יִשָּׂשכָר
yis-saw-kawr'; From H5375 and H7939; he will bring a reward; Jissaskar, a son of Jacob: - Issachar.				
YITRAN	ITHRAN	H3506	יתרן	יִתְרָן
yith-rawn' From H3498; excellent; Jithran, the name of an Edomite and of an Israelite: - Ithran.				
YITZKHAQ	ISAAC	H3327	יצחק	יִצְחָק
yits-khawk'; From H6711; laughter (that is, mockery); Jitschak (or Isaac), son of Abraham: - Isaac. Compare H3446.				
YITZHAR	IZHAR	H3324	יצהר	יִצְהָר
yits-hawr'; From H6671; oil (as producing light); figuratively anointing: - + anointed, oil.				
YIZREEL	JEZREEL	H3157	יזרעאל	יִזְרְעֶאל
yiz-reh-ale'; From H2232 and H410; Elohim will sow; Jizrel, the name of two places in Palestine and of two Yisraelim (Israelites): - Jezreel.				
YOAB	JOAB	H3097	יואב	יוֹאָב
yo-awb'; From H3068 and H1; YAHOWAH-fathered; Joab, the name of three Yisraelim (Israelites): - Joab.				

133

YOBEL	JUBILE	H3104	6૬૧⩊	יוֹבֵל

yo-bale', yo-bale';
Apparently from H2986; the blast of a horn (from its continuous sound);
specifically the signal of the silver trumpets; hence the instrument itself and the
festival thus introduced: - jubile, ram's horn, trumpet.

YOEL	JOEL	H3100	6⩊૧⩊	יוֹאֵל

yo-ale';
From H3068 and H410; YAHOWAH (is his) Elohim; Joel, the name of twelve
Yisraelim (Israelites): - Joel.

YOKEBED	JOCHEBED	H3115	⩤g૪૧⩊	יוֹכֶבֶד

yo-keh'-bed;
From H3068 contracted and H3513; Jehovah-gloried; Jokebed, the mother of
Moses: - Jochebed.

YOKHANAN	JOHN/ JOANNA	H3110	⅁⅁A⅄⩊	יוֹחָנָן

yo-khaw-nawn';
YAHOWAH favored; Jochanan, the name of nine Yisraelim (Israelites): - Johanan.

YOM KIPPUR	DAY OF ATONEMENT	H3725	૧J૪	כִּפֻּר

kippûr, kip-poor';
From H3722; expiation (only in plural): - atonement.

YOM TERUAH	DAY OF BLOWING (TRUMPETS)	H8643	₮0૧૧X	תְּרוּעָה

ter-oo-aw';
From H7321; clamor, that is, acclamation of joy or a battle cry; especially clangor
of trumpets, as an alarum: - alarm, blow (-ing) (of, the) (trumpets), joy, jubile, loud
noise, rejoicing, shout (-ing), (high, joyful) sound (-ing).

YONAH	JONAH/ JONAS	H3124	𐤉𐤅𐤍𐤄	יֹונָה

yo-naw';
a dove; *Jonah*, an Israelite: - Jonah.

YONYAH	JUNIA/ JUNIAS	G2458	𐤉𐤅𐤍𐤉𐤎	יוּנְיֶס

ee-oo-nee'-as;
Of Latin origin; Junias, a Messianic: - Junias.

YOQIM	JOKIM/ ACHIM	H3137	𐤉𐤅𐤒𐤉𐤌	יֹוקִים

yo-keem';
YAHOWAH will raise; A form of H3113; *Jokim*, an Israelite: - Jokim.

YORAM	JORAM/ JORIM	H3141	𐤉𐤅𐤓𐤌	יֹורָם

yo-rawm';
YAHOWAH raised; *Joram*, the name of three Israelites and one Syrian: - Joram.

YOSEPH	JOSEPH	H3130	𐤉𐤅𐤎𐤉	יֹוסֵף

yo-safe';
Future of H3254; let him add (or perhaps simply active participle adding) increase;
Joseph, the name of seven Yisraelim (Israelites): - Joseph. Compare H3084.

YOSHIYAH	JOSIAH/ JOSIAS	H2977	𐤉𐤅𐤔𐤉𐤄	יֹאשִׁיָה

yo-she-yaw', yo-she-yaw'-hoo;
From the same root as H803 and H3050; foundation of YAH; Joshiyah, the name
of two Yisraelim (Israelites): - Josiah.

YOTHAM	JOTHAM/ JOATHAM	H3147	𐤉𐤅𐤓𐤌	יֹותָם

yo-thawm';
From H3068 and H8535; *YAHOWAH* (is) *perfect*; *Jotham*, the name of three
Israelites: - Jotham.

<table>
<tr><td>YUBEL</td><td>JUBAL</td><td>H3106</td><td>𐤉𐤅𐤁𐤋</td><td>יוּבָל</td></tr>
<tr><td colspan="5">yoo-bawl';
From H2986; stream; Jubal, an antediluvian: - Jubal.</td></tr>
<tr><td>YULYA</td><td>JULIA</td><td>G2456</td><td>𐤉𐤅𐤋𐤉𐤀</td><td>יוּלְיָא</td></tr>
<tr><td colspan="5">ee-oo-lee'-ah;
soft haired; Feminine of the same as G2457; Julia, a Messianic woman: - Julia.</td></tr>
<tr><td>YULYOS</td><td>JULIUS</td><td>G2457</td><td>𐤉𐤅𐤋𐤉𐤅𐤎</td><td>יוּלְיוֹס</td></tr>
<tr><td colspan="5">ee-oo'-lee-os;
Of Latin origin; Julius, a centurion: - Julius.</td></tr>
<tr><td>YUSTOS</td><td>JUSTUS</td><td>G2459</td><td>𐤉𐤅𐤎𐤈𐤅𐤎</td><td>יוּסְטוֹס</td></tr>
<tr><td colspan="5">ee-ooce'-tos;
Of Latin origin ("just"); Justus, the name of three Christians: - Justus.</td></tr>
</table>

’

YEHUDI
(JUDITE)

YAHOWAH'S NAME REVEALED

YAHOWAH is The NAME of THE MOST HIGH ELOHIM (GOD) given to the Children of Israel. It is pronounced YA-HO-WAH. His Name means:

HE WAS – HE IS – HE WILL BE
OR
"ETERNAL ONE"

The full revelation of His Set Apart Name is given in the book of Revelation. "Revelation" means to: reveal. Besides revealing His physical appearance (hair like pure wool and feet and skin like unto burnt brass - Rev 1:14-15), The Most High also reveals the mystery of His Name: HE WAS - HE IS -HE WILL BE.

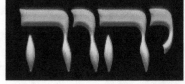

Revelations 1:4
"Yokhanan to the seven Assemblies which are in Asia: Grace be unto you, and shalom, from him WHICH IS, AND WHICH WAS AND WHICH IS TO COME..."

This Scripture reveals YAHOWAH'S Eternal Nature of simultaneously existing within The Past, Present and Future. YAHOWAH'S Name is derived from the Hebrew verb: HAYAH (Strongs H1961).

HAYAH = היה

HAYAH in Hebrew means: "He Was" (past tense). To say "He Is" (present tense) in Hebrew is the word: HOWEH

HOWEH = הוה

Finally, to say "He Will Be" (future tense) in Hebrew is the word: YIHYEH

YIHYEH = יהיה

When The Past, The Present and The Future Are ONE...

When The Eternal Nature of The Most High (Past, Present and Future) are united we have:

YAHOWAH (HAYAH, HOWEH, YIHYEH)

$$\text{יהוה} = \text{היה} + \text{הוה} + \text{יהיה}$$

This Devine Mystery is Revealed 3 More Times...

REVELATION 1:8
"I am Aleph and Taw, saith YAHOWAH, **WHICH IS, AND WHICH WAS AND WHICH IS TO COME**, the Almighty."

REVELATION 4:8
"And the four beasts had each of them six wings about him; and they were full of eyes within: and they rest not day and night, saying, Holy, holy, holy, YAHOWAH ELOHIM Almighty, **WHICH WAS, AND IS, AND IS TO COME.**"

REVELATION 11:17
"Saying, We give thee thanks, O YAHOWAH ELOHIM Almighty, **WHICH ART, AND WAST, AND ART TO COME**; because thou hast taken to thee thy great power, and hast reigned.."

Only by understanding the HEBREW language can we receive the full revelation to unlock the SCRIPTURES and the true meaning of YAHOWAH'S NAME!

ZION

Zion is the seventh letter of the Hebrew alphabet. Symbolically Zion represents a weapon. The numeric value is 7.

HEBREW/ARAMAIC PRONUNCIATION	ENGLISH TRANSLATION	STRONG'S NUMBER	ANCIENT (PALEO) HEBREW	BIBLICAL HEBREW
ZAAWAN	ZAAVAN	H2190	𐤆𐤏𐤅𐤍	זַעֲוָן
zah-av-awn' From H2111; *disquiet*; *Zaavan*, an Idumaean: - Zaavan.				
ZAKAI	ZACCHAEUS	H2140	𐤆𐤊𐤉	זַכַּי
zak-kah'ee; From H2141; pure; Zakkai, a Yisraeli: - Zaccai.				
ZEBULON	ZEBULUN	H2074	𐤆𐤁𐤅𐤋𐤅𐤍	זְבוּלוּן
zeb-oo-loon', From H2082; habitation; Zebulon, a son of Jacob; also his territory and tribe: - Zebulun.				
ZEKARYAH	ZECHARIAH/ ZACHARIAS	H2148	𐤆𐤊𐤓𐤉𐤄	זְכַרְיָה
zek-ar-yaw', zek-ar-yaw'-hoo; From H2142 and H3050; YAH has remembered; Zecaryah, the name of twenty nine Yisraelim: - Zachariah, Zechariah.				
ZEMIRNA	SMYRNA	G4667	𐤆𐤌𐤉𐤓𐤍𐤀	זְמִירְנָא
smoor'-nah; myrrh; The same as G4666; Smyrna, a place in Asia Minor: - Smyrna.				
ZERAKH	ZARAH/ ZERAH/ ZARA	H2225	𐤆𐤓𐤇	זֶרַח
zeh'-rakh; From H2224; a *rising* of light: - rising.				
ZERUBABEL	ZERUBBABEL/ ZOROBABEL	H2216	𐤆𐤓𐤁𐤁𐤋	זְרֻבָּבֶל

Z- INDEX

HEBREW/ARAMAIC PRONUNCIATION	ENGLISH TRANSLATION	STRONG'S NUMBER	ANCIENT (PALEO) HEBREW	BIBLICAL HEBREW
zer-oob-baw-bel'; From H2215 and H894; *descended of* (that is, from) *Babylon*, that is, born there; *Zerubbabel*, an Israelite: - Zerubbabel.				

♪ ZAMMAR
(Singer)

"Then said I, Lo, I come: in the volume of the book it is written of me, I delight to do thy will, O my ELOHIM." - Hebrews 10:7

BOOKS OF THE NEW TESTAMENT

MATTHEW/MATTITYAHU: **GIFT OF YAH**
MARK/MARQOS: **A DEFENSE**
LUKE/LUQAS: **LIGHT GIVING**
JOHN/YOKHANAN: **GRACE OF YAHOWAH**
ACTS/MA'ASAY: **ACT**
ROMANS/ROMIM: **ROMAN?**
1 CORINTHIANS/QORINTIM RISHON: **SATIATED**
2 CORINTHIANS/QORINTIM SHENI: **SATIATED**
GALATIANS/GALATIM: **FOREIGNER**
EPHESIANS/EPHESIM: **PERMITTED**
PHILLIPIANS/PHILIPIM: **LOVER OF HORSES**
COLOSSIANS/QOLASIM: **GIGANTIC**
1 THESSALONIANS/TESSALONIQIM RISHON: **VICTORY OF FALSITY**
2 THESSALONIANS/TESSALONIQIM SHENI: **VICTORY OF FALSITY**

1 TIMOTHY/TIMOTHEOS RISHON: **DEAR TO ELOHIM**
2 TIMOTHY/TIMOTHEOS SHENI: **DEAR TO ELOHIM**
TITUS/TITOS: **NURSE**
PHILEMON/PHILIMON: **ONE WHO KISSES**
HEBREWS/IBRIM: **FROM BEYOND**
JAMES/YA'AQOB: **SUPPLANTER**
1 PETER/KEPHA RISHON: **ROCK**
2 PETER/KEPHA SHENI: **ROCK**
1 JOHN/YOKHANAN RISHON: **GRACE OF YAHOWAH**
2 JOHN/YOKHANAN SHENI: **GRACE OF YAHOWAH**
3 JOHN/YOKHANAN SHELISHI: **GRACE OF YAHOWAH**
JUDE/YEHUDAH: **PRAISE**
REVELATION/HITGALUT: **REVEALED**

THE HIDDEN PROPHECY REVEALED

He is a gift of YAH and a defense that gives light. An act of YAHOWAH'S grace to satiate those in Rome. He has permitted the foreigners, who love horses and have colossal victories from false-hood to become dear to ELOHIM. Dear to ELOHIM as a nurse who kisses the Hebrews. The Rock of Ya'aqob and the Grace of YAHOWAH has been revealed to Yehudah!

Virtuous Women of YAH

We all hear about important people in the bible like King David, and Elijah the prophet. But what about the women? How are women important to the nation?

When you start to understand the role of a woman, they you'll recognize how important she really is. She submits to her husband and the proper order that YAHOWAH has ordained. She raises and teaches the children, and is a help meet/supporter of her husband.

By her submitting, she brings peace inside the home. In most families, the man and the woman are always arguing. Even when watching TV, the husband and wife always argue like cats and dogs. When a woman always combats her husband, there is no peace. The opposite of peace is chaos. By her respecting and submitting to her husband, she creates a bond of peace, happiness, trust, and love. Let's examine a woman who followed her role perfectly.

Genesis 12:11-13 And it came to pass, when he was come near to enter into Mitzraim, that he said unto Sarai his wife, Behold now, I know that thou art a fair wom¬an to look upon: 12 Therefore it shall come to pass, when the Mitz¬rim shall see thee, that they shall say, This is his wife: and they will kill me, but they will save thee alive. 13 Say, I pray thee, thou art my sister: that it may be well with me for thy sake; and my soul shall live because of thee.

It Sarah didn't submit, she could've gotten Abraham killed. It was so easy for her to forsake Abraham, to become the queen of Egypt. If Abraham died, we wouldn't exist! Imagine if Sarah was the opposite of a virtuous woman, and started a full blown argument. She would've created a number of problems. For starters, they'd have nowhere to go because there was a famine during that time, and if they went into Egypt, Abraham would be killed. On top of that, they'd feel bitter towards each other, depressed, and hungry. Because Sarah was virtuous, she is as noble as King David. She is a role model for women throughout every generation of how a woman should operate.

Women also have a powerful influence on men. Have you ever been somewhere and seen a man look straight up depressed? It's most likely because of a woman he has to deal with. That's why it's important for women to be virtuous, because they can influence the man to be righteous as well.

1 Peter 3:1 Likewise, ye wives, be in subjection to your own husbands; that, if any obey not the word, they also may without the word be won by the conversation of the wives

Even a Abigail saved King David's life. A good woman can be as strong as King David, but it's a different kind of strength. The strength she has is virtue, peace, kindness, and wisdom.

Proverbs 31:25 Strength and honour are her clothing; and she shall rejoice in time to come.

א

AHAVAH (LOVE)

Feminine of H158 and meaning the same: - love. A primitive root; to have affection for (sexually or otherwise): - (be-) love (-d, -ly, -r), like, friend.

H160

"This is my commandment, That ye love one another, as I have loved you." - John 15:12

HEBREW/ARAMAIC PRONUNCIATION	ENGLISH TRANSLATION	STRONG'S NUMBER	ANCIENT (PALEO) HEBREW	BIBLICAL HEBREW
ABI	ABI	H21	ꙮ	אֲבִי

ab-ee'
From H1; *fatherly*; *Abi*, Hezekiah's mother: - Abi.

| ABIGAYIL | ABIGAIL | H26 | | אֲבִיגַיִל |

ab-ee-gah'yil, ab-ee-gal';
From H1 and H1524; *father (that is source) of joy*; *Abigail* or *Abigal*, the name of two Israelitesses: - Abigal

| ABISHAG | ABISHAG | H49 | | אֲבִישַׁג |

ab-ee-shag'
From H1 and H7686; *father of error* (that is, *blundering*); *Abishag*, a concubine of David: - Abishag.

| ABITAL | ABITAL | H37 | | אֲבִיטַל |

ab-ee-tal'
From H1 and H2919; *father of dew* (that is, *fresh*); *Abital*, a wife of King David: - Abital.

| ABIYAH | ABIJAH ABIA ABIAH | H29 | | אֲבִיָּה |

ab-ee-yaw', ab-ee-yaw'-hoo;
From H1 and H3050; *YAHOWAH is my Father*; *father* (that is *worshipper*) *of Jah*; *Abijah*, the name of several Israelite men and two Israelitesses: - Abiah, Abijah.

| ADAH | ADAH | H5710 | | עָדָה |

aw-daw';
A primitive root; to *advance*, that is, *pass* on or *continue*; causatively to *remove*; specifically to *bedeck* (that is, bring an ornament upon): - adorn, deck (self), pass by, take away.

| AKHINOAM | AHINOAM | H293 | | אֲחִינֹעַם |

akh-ee-no'-am
From H251 and H5278; *brother of pleasantness*; *Achinoam*, the name of two Israelitesses: - Ahinoam.

A- WOMEN'S INDEX

HEBREW/ARAMAIC PRONUNCIATION	ENGLISH TRANSLATION	STRONG'S NUMBER	ANCIENT (PALEO) HEBREW	BIBLICAL HEBREW
AKHLAI	AHLAI	H304	ילחא	אַחְלָי
akh-lah'ee The same as H305; *wishful*; *Achlai*, the name of an Israelitess and of an Israelite: - Ahlai.				
AKSAH	ACHSAH	H5915	הסכע	עַכְסָה
ak-saw' Feminine of H5914; *anklet*; *Aksah*, an Israelitess: - Achsah.				
ANAH	ANAH	H6034	הנע	עֲנָה
an-aw'; Probably form H6030; an *answer*; *Anah*, the name of two Edomites and one Edomitess: - Anah.				
APHIYAH	APPHIA	G682	היפא	אַפִּיָּה
ap-fee'-a Probably of foreign origin; *Apphia*, a woman of Colossae: - Apphia.				
ASENATH	ASENATH	H621	תנסא	אָסְנַת
aw-se-nath' Of Egyptian derivation; *Asenath*, the wife of Joseph: - Asenath.				
ATARAH	ATARAH	H5851	הרטע	עֲטָרָה
at-aw-raw' a *crown*:; *Atarah*, an Israelitess: - Atarah.				
ATHALYAH	ATHALIAH	H6271	היֿלֿתֿע	עֲתַלְיָה
ath-al-yaw', ath-al-yaw'-hoo; From the same as H6270 and H3050; YAH has constrained; Athalyah, the name of an Israelitess and two Yisraelim: - Athaliah.				
AYPHAH	EPHAH	H5891	הפיע	עֵיפָה

HEBREW/ARAMAIC PRONUNCIATION	ENGLISH TRANSLATION	STRONG'S NUMBER	ANCIENT (PALEO) HEBREW	BIBLICAL HEBREW
ay-faw' The same as H5890; *Ephah*, the name of a son of Midian, and of the region settled by him; also of an Israelite and of an Israelitess: - Ephah.				
AZUBAH	AZUBAH	H5806	ﬤﬢשׁﬡﬦ	עֲזוּבָה
az-oo-baw' *desertion*; *Azubah*, the name of two Israelitesses: - Azubah.				

BETH (TENT)

The letter Beth in ancient (paleo) Hebrew is symbolized as an open tent. Tents were used by the Israelites to celebrate the Feast of Tabernacles in the wilderness.

"Enlarge the place of thy tent, and let them stretch forth the curtains of thine habitations..." - Isaiah 54:2

HEBREW/ARAMAIC PRONUNCIATION	ENGLISH TRANSLATION	STRONG'S NUMBER	ANCIENT (PALEO) HEBREW	BIBLICAL HEBREW
BA'ARA	BAARA	H1199	⨯⟍◯𝑔	בַּעֲרָא

bah-ar-aw'
From H1198; *brutish*; *Baara*, an Israelitish woman: - Baara.

| BASMATH BASEMATH | BASHEMATH | H1315 | ⨯𝑦w𝑔 | בָּשְׂמַת |

bos-math';
Feminine of the second form of H1314; *fragrance*; smell, spice, sweet (odour);
Bosmath, the name of a wife of Esau, and of a dughter of Solomon: - Bashemath,
Basmath.

| BATHSHEBA | BATHSHEBA | H1339 | ○𝑔w-⨯𝑔 | בַּת־שֶׁבַע |

bath-sheh'-bah
From H1323 and H7651 (in the sense of H7650); *daughter of an oath*; *BathSheba*,
the mother of Solomon: - Bath-sheba.

| BERNIQAH | BERNICE | G959 | ℨ𝑞𝑉𝑦⟍𝑔 | בֶּרְנִיקָה |

ber-nee'-kay;
From a provincial form of G5342 and G3529; *victorious*; Bernice, a member of the
Herodian family: - Bernice.

| BILHAH | BILHAH | H1090 | ℨℨ6𝑔 | בִּלְהָה |

bil-haw'
From H1089; *timid*; *Bilhah*, the name of one of Jacob's concubines; also of a place
in Palestine: - Bilhah.

| BITHYAH | BITHIAH | H1332 | ℨ𝑉⨯𝑔 | בִּתְיָה |

bith-yaw'
From H1323 and H3050; *daughter* (that is, worshipper) *of YAH*; *Bithjah*, an
Egyptian woman: - Bithiah.

ב BETULAH
(Virgin)

ד

DALET (DOOR)

From H1802; something swinging, that is, the valve of a door: - door (two-leaved), gate, leaf, lid.

H1817

"Blessed is the man that heareth me, watching daily at my gates, waiting at the posts of my doors." - Proverbs 8:34

HEBREW/ARAMAIC PRONUNCIATION	ENGLISH TRANSLATION	STRONG'S NUMBER	ANCIENT (PALEO) HEBREW	BIBLICAL HEBREW
DAMARIS	DAMARIS	G1152	‡א⅄ש◿	דְּמָרִיס

dam'-ar-is
Probably from the base of G1150; perhaps *gentle*; *Damaris*, an Athenian woman: - Damaris.

| DEBORAH | DEBORAH | H1683 | ⅂⅄⅄ש◿ | דְּבוֹרָה |

deb-o-raw', deb-o-raw'
the *bee* (from its *systematic* instincts): - bee.; *Deborah*, the name of two Hebrewesses: - Deborah.

| DELILAH | DELILAH | H1807 | ⅂6א6◿ | דְּלִילָה |

del-ee-law'
From H1809; *languishing*: - Delilah, a Philistine woman: - Delilah.

| DINAH | DINAH | H1783 | ⅂ℑא◿ | דִּינָה |

dee-naw'
Feminine of H1779; *justice*; *Dinah*, the daughter of Jacob: - Dinah.

| DRUSILLAH | DRUSILLA | G1409 | ⅂⅂6g | דְּרוּסִלָּה |

droo'-sil-lah
A feminine diminutive of *Drusus* (a Roman name); *Drusilla*, a member of the Herodian family: - Drusilla.

| EBHODIYAH | EUODIAS | G2136 | ℑ⅄◿⅄⅂ℑא | אֲבְהוֹדִיָה |

yoo-od-ee'-ah;
From the same as G2137; *fine travelling*; *Euodia*, a Messianic woman: - Euodias.

| EGLAH | EGLAH | H5698 | w6ℑo | עֶגְלָה |

eg-law'
The same as H5697; *Eglah*, a wife of David: - Eglah.

| ELISHEBA | ELISABETH | H472 | 0gwא6א | אֱלִישֶׁבַע |

HEBREW/ARAMAIC PRONUNCIATION	ENGLISH TRANSLATION	STRONG'S NUMBER	ANCIENT (PALEO) HEBREW	BIBLICAL HEBREW
el-ee-sheh'-bah From H410 and H7651 (in the sense of H7650); *God of* (the) *oath*; *Elisheba*, the wife of Aaron: - Elisheba.				
ESTHER	ESTHER	H635	⟨×‡⟨	אֶסְתֵּר
es-tare'; Of Persian derivation; *star*, *Ester*, the Yehudim heroine: - Esther				
GOMER	GOMER	H1586	⟨℈⟨	גֹּמֶר
go'-mer From H1584; *completion*; *Gomer*, the name of a son of Japheth and of his descendants; also of a *Hebrewess:* - Gomer.				

ה
HEH (WINDOW)

The Letter Heh symbolizes "window", to "behold" and to "look." A primitive particle; lo!: - behold, lo.

H1887

"And it came to pass at the end of forty days, that Noakh opened the window of the ark which he had made:" - Genesis 8:6

HEBREW/ARAMAIC PRONUNCIATION	ENGLISH TRANSLATION	STRONG'S NUMBER	ANCIENT (PALEO) HEBREW	BIBLICAL HEBREW
HADASSAH	HADASSAH	H1919	ヨキ△ヨ	הֲדַסָּה

had-as-saw'
myrtle: - myrtle (tree); *Hadassah* (or Esther): - Hadassah.

| HAGAR | HAGAR AGAR | H1904 | ᑫリヨ | הָגָר |

haw-gawr'
flight; *Hagar*, the mother of Ishmael: - Hagar.

| HA'MOLEKETH MOLEKETH | HAMMOLEKETH | H4447 | ×9ᒪᕿ | הַמֹּלֶכֶת |

mo-leh'-keth
Feminine active participle of H4427; *queen*; *Moleketh*, an Israelitess, (including the article): - Hammoleketh [includ. the article.]

| HODIYAH | HODIAH | H1940 | ᒪᐯ△ᕿᑫ | הוֹדִיָה |

ho-dee-yaw'
A form for the feminine of H3064;a *Jehudite* (that is, Judaite or Jew), or descendant of Jehudah (that is, Judah) a *Jewess:* - Hodiah.

| HORODYAH | HERODIAS | G2266 | ᒪᐯ△ᕿᕿᑫ | הוֹרוֹדִיָה |

hay-ro-dee-as';
From G2264; Herodias, heroic, a woman of the Herodian family: - Herodias.

| IYZEBEL | JEZEBEL | H348 | ᒪ9ᒪᐯ⋏ | אִיזֶבֶל |

jez'-e-bel 'izebhel;
"unexalted," "unhusbanded"; the wife of king Ahab:

| KAZBIY | COZBI | H3579 | ᐯ9ᒪy | כָּזְבִּי |

koz-bee'
From H3576; *false*; *Cozbi*, a Midianitess: - Cozbi.

| KHAGITH | HAGGITH | H2294 | ×ᐯᎶᗷ | חַגִּית |

khag-gheeth'
Feminine of H2291; *festive*; *Chaggith*, a wife of David: - Haggith.

HEBREW/ARAMAIC PRONUNCIATION	ENGLISH TRANSLATION	STRONG'S NUMBER	ANCIENT (PALEO) HEBREW	BIBLICAL HEBREW
KHAMUTAL	HAMUTAL	H2537	6⊗৭ﬦﬧ	חֲמוּטַל

kham-oo-tal', kham-ee-tal'
From H2524 and H2919; *father in law of dew*; *Chamutal* or *Chamital*, an Israelitess: - Hamutal.

| KHANAH | HANNAH ANNA | H2584 | ৭ﬠﬧ | חַנָּה |

khan-naw'
From H2603; *favored*; *Channah*, an Israelitess: - Hannah.

| KHAWAH | EVE | H2332 | w6৭o | עֶגְלָה |

khaw-waw'
Causative from H2331; *lifegiver*; *Chavvah* (or Eve), the first woman: - Eve.

| KHELAH | HELAH | H2458 | ﬗﬥ6ﬧ | חֶלְאָה |

khel-aw'
properly *disease*; hence *rust:* - scum.; *Chelah*, an Israelitess: - Helah.

| KHEPH'TZIBAH | HEPHZIBAH | H2657 | ৭9-ﬗﬣﬧ | חֶפְצִי בָהּ |

khef-tsee' baw
From H2656 with suffixes; *my delight* (is) *in her*; *Cheptsibah*, a fanciful name for Palestine: - Hephzi-bah.

| KHODESH | HODESH | H2321 | w△ﬧ | חֹדֶשׁ |

kho'-desh
renewed month; *Chodesh*, an Israelitess: - Hodesh.

| KHULDAH | HULDAH | H2468 | ﬗ△6ﬧ | חֻלְדָּה |

khool-daw'
a *weasel* (from its *gliding* motion): - weasel.; *Chuldah*, an Israelitess: - Huldah.

| KHUSHIM | HUSHIM | H2366 | ﬦ﬩wﬧﬧ | חוּשִׁים |

khoo-sheem' (all forms)
Plural from H2363; *hasters*; *Chushim*, the name of three Israelites: - Hushim.

HEBREW/ARAMAIC PRONUNCIATION	ENGLISH TRANSLATION	STRONG'S NUMBER	ANCIENT (PALEO) HEBREW	BIBLICAL HEBREW
KLOAH	CHLOE	G5514	𐤊𐤋𐤅𐤀𐤄	כְּלוֹאָה

khlo'-ay

Feminine of apparently a primary word; "green"; *Chloe*, a Christian female: - Chloe.

כ KALLAH
(Bride)

LEKHEM (BREAD)

From H3898; food (for man or beast), especially bread, or grain (for making it): - ([shew-]) bread, X eat, food, fruit, loaf, meat, victuals. See also H1036
H3899

"And YAHOSHUA said unto them, I am the bread of life: he that cometh to me shall never hunger; and he that believeth on me shall never thirst." - John 6:35

HEBREW/ARAMAIC PRONUNCIATION	ENGLISH TRANSLATION	STRONG'S NUMBER	ANCIENT (PALEO) HEBREW	BIBLICAL HEBREW
LEAH	LEAH	H3812	ヲ⊀6	לֵאָה

lay-aw'
From H3811; *weary*; *Leah*, a wife of Jacob: - Leah.

| LOIS | LOIS | G3090 | ₮Ⴎ⊀ꟼ6 | לוֹאִיס |

lo-ece'
agreeable; *Lois*, a Christian woman: - Lois.

| LO-RUKHAMAH | LO-RUHAMAH | H3819 | ヲﾘꟼꟼ-⊀6 | לוֹ–רֻחָמָה |

lo roo-khaw-maw'
From H3808 and H7355; *not pitied*; *lo Ruchamah*, the symbolical name of a son of Hosea: - Lo-ruhamah.

| LUD | LYDIA | H3865 | △ꟼ6 | לוּד |

lood
Probably of foreign derivation; *Lud*, the name of two nations: - Lud, Lydia.

| MA'AKATH | MAACHAH | H4601 | ヲYOꟼ | מַעֲכָה |

mah-ak-aw', mah-ak-awth'
From H4600; *depression*; *Maakah* (or *Maakath*), the name of a place in Syria, also of a Mesopotamian, of three Israelites, and of four Israelitesses and one Syrian woman: - Maachah, Maachathites. See also H1038.

| MAKHLAH | MAHALAH | H4244 | ヲ6月ꟼ | מַחְלָה |

makh-law'
From H2470; *sickness*; *Machlah*, the name apparently of two Israelitesses: - Mahlah.

| MARA | MARA | H4755 | ⊀ꟼꟼ | מָרָא |

maw-raw'
For H4751 feminine; *bitter*; *Mara*, a symbolical name of Naomi: - Mara.

| MARTHA | MARTHA | H4755 | ⊀X9ꟼ | מָרְתָא |

HEBREW/ARAMAIC PRONUNCIATION	ENGLISH TRANSLATION	STRONG'S NUMBER	ANCIENT (PALEO) HEBREW	BIBLICAL HEBREW

mar'-thah
Probably of Chaldee origin (meaning *mistress*); *Martha*, a Christian woman: - Martha.

| MATRED | MATRED | H4308 | ◁٩⊗ꟹ | מַטְרֵד |

mat-rade'
From H2956; *propulsive*; *Matred*, an Edomitess: - Matred.

| MEHETABEL | MEHETABEL | H4105 | 6≮9⊗ᐯᒿꟹ | מְהֵיטַבְאֵל |

meh-hay-tab-ale'
From H3190 (augmented) and H410; *bettered of God*; *Mehetabel*, the name of an Edomitish man and woman: - Mehetabeel, Mehetabel.

| MERAB | MERAB | H4764 | ᓂꟹ | מֵרַב |

may-rawb'
From H7231; *increase*; *Merab*, a daughter of Saul: - Merab.

| MESHULLEMETH | MESHULLEMETH | H4922 | ✕ꟹ6Wꟹ | מְשֻׁלֶּמֶת |

mesh-ool-leh'-meth
allied; *Meshullemeth*, an Israelitess: - Meshullemeth.

| MILKAH | MILCAH | H4435 | ᒿꟿ6ꟹ | מִלְכָּה |

mil-kaw'
A form of H4436; *queen*; *Milcah*, the name of a Hebrewess and of an Israelite: - Milcah.

| MIKAL | MICHAL | H4324 | 6ꟿᐯꟹ | מִיכָל |

me-kawl';
from H3201; properly, a container, i.e. a streamlet:—brook..

| MIKAYAH | MICHAIAH | H4320 | ᒿᐯ ꟿᐯꟹ | מִיכָיְה |

me-kaw-yaw'
From H4310 and (the prefixed derivation from) H3588 and H3050; *who* (is) *like Jah?*; *Micajah*, the name of two Israelites: - Micah, Michaiah. Compare H4318.

HEBREW/ARAMAIC PRONUNCIATION	ENGLISH TRANSLATION	STRONG'S NUMBER	ANCIENT (PALEO) HEBREW	BIBLICAL HEBREW
MIRYAM	MARY MIRIAM	H4813	𐤌𐤉𐤓𐤌	מִרְיָם

meer-yawm'
From H4805; *rebelliously*; *Mirjam*, the name of two Israelitesses: - Miriam.

מ MAYIM
(water)

NAKHASH (SERPENT)

From H5172; a snake (from its hiss): - serpent. A primitive root; properly to hiss, that is, whisper a (magic) spell; generally to prognosticate: - X certainly, divine, enchanter, (use) X enchantment, learn by experience, X indeed, diligently observe.

H5172

"Now the serpent was more subtil than any beast of the field which YAHOWAH ELOHIM had made." - John 6:35

HEBREW/ARAMAIC PRONUNCIATION	ENGLISH TRANSLATION	STRONG'S NUMBER	ANCIENT (PALEO) HEBREW	BIBLICAL HEBREW
NA'AMAH	NAAMAH	H5279	𐤉𐤏𐤌𐤄	נַעֲמָה

nah-am-aw'
Feminine of H5277; *pleasantness*; *Naamah*, the name of an antediluvian woman, of an Ammonitess, and of a place in Palestine: - Naamah.

| NA'AMI | NAOMI | H5281 | 𐤉𐤌𐤏𐤍 | נָעֳמִי |

no-om-ee'
From H5278; *pleasant*; *Noomi*, an Israelitess: - Naomi.

| NA'ARAH | NAARAH | H5292 | 𐤉𐤏𐤓𐤄 | נַעֲרָה |

nah-ar-aw'
a *girl* (from infancy to adolescence): - damsel, maid (-en), young (woman); *Naarah*, the name of an Israelitess, and of a place in Palestine: - Naarah, Naarath.

| NEKHUSHTA | NEHUSHTA | H5179 | 𐤀𐤕𐤔𐤇𐤍 | נְחֻשְׁתָּא |

nekh-oosh-taw'
From H5178; *copper*; *Nechushta*, an Israelitess: - Nehushta.

| NOADYAH | NOADIAH | H5129 | 𐤄𐤉𐤃𐤏𐤅𐤍 | נוֹעַדְיָה |

no-ad-yaw'
From H3259 and H3050; *convened of YAH*; *Noadjah*, the name of an Israelite, and a false prophetess: - Noadiah.

| PARSIS | PERSIS | G4069 | 𐤉𐤒𐤎𐤓𐤐 | פֶּרְסִיס |

per-sece'
A *Persian* woman; *Persis*, a Christian female: - Persis.

| PENINAH | PENINNAH | H6444 | 𐤉𐤍𐤍𐤐 | פְּנִנָּה |

pen-in-naw'
probably a *pearl* (as *round*): - ruby.; *Peninnah*, an Israelitess: - Peninnah.

| PHUBI | PHEBE | G5402 | 𐤉𐤁𐤉𐤐 | פוּבִי |

HEBREW/ARAMAIC PRONUNCIATION	ENGLISH TRANSLATION	STRONG'S NUMBER	ANCIENT (PALEO) HEBREW	BIBLICAL HEBREW
foy'-bay; Feminine of Phoibos (bright; probably akin to the base of G5457); Phaebe, a Messianic woman: - Phebe.				
PRISQELAH	PRISCILLA	G4252	𐤉𐤋𐤒𐤎𐤓𐤐	פְּרִיסְקְלָה
pris'-cil-lah; Diminutive of G4251; ancient; Priscilla (that is, little Prisca), a Messianic woman: - Priscilla.				
PUAH	PUAH	H6326	𐤄𐤏𐤅𐤐	פּוּעָה
poo-aw' From an unused root meaning to *glitter*; *brilliancy*; *Puah*, an Israelitess: - Puah.				

QARA (READ)

To call out to (that is, properly address by name, but used in a wide variety of applications): - bewray [self], that are bidden, call (for, forth, self, upon), cry (unto), (be) famous, guest, invite, mention, (give) name, preach, (make) proclaim (-ation), pronounce, publish, read, renowned, say.

H7121

"And he took the book of the covenant, and read in the audience of the people: and they said, All that YAHOWAH hath said will we do, and be obedient." -Exodus 24:7

HEBREW/ARAMAIC PRONUNCIATION	ENGLISH TRANSLATION	STRONG'S NUMBER	ANCIENT (PALEO) HEBREW	BIBLICAL HEBREW
QEREN-HAPHUK	KEREN-HAPPUCH	H5279	𐤟𐤟𐤟	קֶרֶן־הַפּוּךְ

keh'-ren hap-pook'

From <u>H7161</u> and <u>H6320</u>; *horn of cosmetic*; *Keren-hap-Puk*, one of Job's daughters: - Keren-happuch.

| QETURAH | KETURAH | H6989 | 𐤟𐤟𐤟 | קְטוּרָה |

ket-oo-raw'

Feminine passive participle of <u>H6999</u>; *perfumed*; *Keturah*, a wife of Abraham: - Keturah.

| QETZIAH | KEZIA | H7103 | 𐤟𐤟𐤟 | קְצִיעָה |

kets-ee-aw'

cassia (as *peeled*; plural the *bark*): - cassia.; *Ketsiah*, a daughter of Job: - Kezia.

| RAKHAB | RAHAB | H5129 | 𐤟𐤟𐤟 | רָחָב |

raw-khawb'

broad, large, at liberty, wide.; *proud*; *Rachab*, a Canaanitess: - Rahab.

| RAKHEL | RACHEL | H7354 | 𐤟𐤟𐤟 | רָחֵל |

raw-khale'

a *ewe* (the *females* being the predominant element of a flock), (as a good *traveller*): - ewe, sheep.; *Rachel*, a wife of Jacob: - Rachel.

| REUMAH | REUMAH | H7208 | 𐤟𐤟𐤟 | רְאוּמָה |

reh-oo-maw'

Feminine passive participle of <u>H7213</u>; *raised*; *Reumah*, a Syrian woman: - Reumah.

| RIBQAH | REBEKAH | H7259 | 𐤟𐤟𐤟 | רִבְקָה |

rib-kaw'

ensnarer; to *clog* by tying up the fetlock; *fettering* (by beauty); *Ribkah*, the wife of Isaac: - Rebekah.

| RITZPAH | RIZPAH | H7532 | 𐤟𐤟𐤟 | רִצְפָּה |

HEBREW/ARAMAIC PRONUNCIATION	ENGLISH TRANSLATION	STRONG'S NUMBER	ANCIENT (PALEO) HEBREW	BIBLICAL HEBREW
rits-paw' a hot *stone*; also a tessellated *pavement:* - live coal, pavement.; *Ritspah*, an Israelitess: - Rizpah.				
RODI	RHODA	G5402	𐤓𐤄𐤃𐤀	רוֹדִי
hrod'-ay Probably for rhod (a *rose*); *Rode*, a servant girl: - Rhoda.				
RUTH	RUTH	H7327	𐤓𐤅𐤕	רוּת
rooth a female *associate*; generally an *additional* one: - + another, mate, neighbour.; *friend*; *Ruth*, a Moabitess: - Ruth.				

RA'AH
(Shepherd)

SEH (Lamb)

Probably from H7582 through the idea of pushing out to graze; a member of a flock, that is, a sheep or goat: - (lesser, small) cattle, ewe, lamb, sheep.

H7716

"And looking upon YAHOSHUA as he walked,he saith, Behold the Lamb of ELOHIM!"-John 1:36

HEBREW/ARAMAIC PRONUNCIATION	ENGLISH TRANSLATION	STRONG'S NUMBER	ANCIENT (PALEO) HEBREW	BIBLICAL HEBREW
SARAH	SARAH	H8283	ⅎ٩w	שָׂרָה

saw-raw'
a *mistress*, that is, female noble: - lady, princess, queen.; *Sarah*, Abraham's wife: - Sarah.

| SARAI | SARAI | H8297 | ⱴ٩w | שָׂרַי |

saw-rah'ee
princess; *dominative*; *Sarai*, the wife of Abraham: - Sarai.

| SERAKH | SERAH | H8294 | ⱻ٩w | שֶׂרַח |

seh'-rakh
remnant; *superfluity*; *Serach*, an Israelitess: - Sarah, Serah.

| SHAPHIRAH | SAPPHIRA | G4551 | ⅎ٩ⱴ ❋w | שַׁפִּירָה |

sap-fi'-ray
a "sapphire" or *lapis-lazuli* gem: - sapphire.; *Sapphire*, an Israelitess: - Sapphira.

| SHE'ERAH | SHERAH | H7609 | ⅎ٩⅍w | שְׁאֵרָה |

sheh-er-aw'
female *kindred* by blood: - near kinswomen.; *Sheerah*, an Israelitess: - Sherah.

| SHELOMITH | SALOME | H7965 | ×ⱴ❋6w | שְׁלֹמִית |

sal-o'-may
From H7999; *safe*, that is, (figuratively) *well*, *happy*, *friendly*; also (abstractly) *welfare*, that is, health, prosperity, peace: -   X do, familiar, X fare, favour, + friend, X greet, (good) health, (X perfect, such as be at) peace (-able, -ably), prosper (-ity, -ous), rest, safe (-ly), salute, welfare, (X all is, be) well, X wholly.; *Salome* (that is, *Shelomah*), an Israelitess: - Salome.

| SHIMATH | SHIMEATH | H8100 | ×o❋w | שִׁמְעָת |

shim-awth'
annunciation; something *heard*, that is, a *sound, rumor, announcement*; abstractly *audience*: - bruit, fame, hear (-ing), loud, report, speech, tidings; *Shimath*, an Ammonitess: - Shimath.

HEBREW/ARAMAIC PRONUNCIATION	ENGLISH TRANSLATION	STRONG'S NUMBER	ANCIENT (PALEO) HEBREW	BIBLICAL HEBREW
SHIMRITH	SHIMRITH	H8116	×⩗⩛𐤔w	שִׁמְרִית

shim-reeth'
Feminine of H8113; *female guard*; *Shimrith*, a Moabitess: - Shimrith.

| SHIPHRAH | SHIPHRAH | H8236 | ⩣⩑𐤔w | שִׁפְרָה |

shif-raw'
brightness; The same as H8235; *Shiphrah*, an Israelitess: - Shiphrah.

| SHOMER | SHOMER | H7763 | ⩑𐤌𐤔w | שׁוֹמֵר |

sho-mare', sho-mare'
Active participle of H8104; *keeper*; *Shomer*, the name of two Israelites: - Shomer.

| SHOSHANNAH | SUSANNA | H7799 | ⩣𐤍w𐤔w | שׁוֹשַׁנָּה |

sho-shan-naw'
From H7797; a *lily* (from its *whiteness*), as a flower or architectural ornament; also a (straight) *trumpet* (from the *tubular* shape): - lily, Shoshannim.

| SHUA | SHUA | H7770 | O⩑w | שׁוּעַ |

shoo'-ah
cry, riches; The same as H7769; *shua*, a Canaanite: - Shua, Shuah.

| SUNTIKI | SYNTYCHE | G4941 | ⩗𐤉𐤍⊗⩛⩣𐤚 | סוּנְטִיכִי |

soon-too'-khay
From G4940; an *accident*; *Syntyche*, a Christian female: - Syntyche.

שׁ SHEMESH

(Sun)

TEN COMMANDMENTS IN BIBLICAL HEBREW

אנכי יהוה אלהיך אשר הוצאתיך מארץ מצרים מבית עבדים:

לא יהיה–לך אלהים אחרים על פני: ANOKI YAHOWAH ELOHAY-KA .1

ASHER HOTZAYTI-KA M'ARETZ MITZRAYIM M'BAYT ABADIM: LO YIYEH-LEKA ELOHIM AKHARIM AL-PANAI

לא תעשה–לך פסל וכל–תמונה אשר בשמים ממעל ואשר
בארץ מתחת ואשר במים מתחת לארץ: לא–תשתחוה להם ולא
תעבדם כי אנכי יהוה אלהיך אל קנא פקד עון אבת על–בנים
על–שלשים ועל–רבעים לשנאי: ועשה חסד לאלפים לאהבי
ולשמרי מצותי: ASHER .2 LO TA'ASEH-LEKA PHESEL W'KAL-TEMUNAH

BA-SHAMAYIM MI-MA'AL WA-ASHER BA-ARETZ MI-TAKHAT WA-ASHER BA-MAYIM MI-TAKHAT LA-ARETZ: LO-TISHTAKHEWEH LAHEM W'LO TA'ABDEM KI ANOKI YAHOWAH ELOHAY-KA EL QANA POQED AON ABOTE AL-BANIM AL-SHILESHIM W'AL-RIBAYIM L-SONAI: W'OSEH KHESED LA-ALAPHIM L'OHABAI UL-SHOMRAY MITZWOTAI:

TEN COMMANDMENTS IN BIBLICAL HEBREW

לא תשא את–שם–יהוה אלהיך לשוא כי לא ינקה יהוה את

אשר–ישא את–שמו לשוא:

3. LO TISA ET-SHEM-YAHOWAH ELOHAY-KA:
LA-SHAW KI LO YENAQEH YAHOWAH ET ASHER-YISA ET-SHEMO LA-SHAW:

זכור את–יום השבת לקדשו: ששת ימים תעבד ועשית

כל–מלאכתך: ויום השביעי שבת ליהוה אלהיך לא–תעשה

כל–מלאכה אתה ובנך–ובתך עבדך ואמתך ובהמתך וגרך אשר

בשעריך: כי ששת–ימים עשה יהוה את–השמים ואת–הארץ

את–הים ואת–כל–אשר–בם וינח ביום השביעי על–כן ברך

יהוה את–יום השבת ויקדשהו:

4. ZAKOR ET-YOM HA-SHABBAT
LE-QADSHO: SHESHET YAMIM TA'ABODE W'ASITA KAL-ME-LAK-TEKA: W'YOM
HA-SHEBI'EE SHABBAT LA-YAHOWAH ELOHAY-KA LO-TA'ASEH KAL-MELAKAH ATAH
UBIN-KA- UBITEKA ABDE-KA WA-AMAT-KA U'BEHEM-TEKA W'GER-KA ASHER
BISHARAY-KA: KI SHESHET - YAMIM ASAH YAHOWAH ET-HA-SHAMAYIM
W'ET-HA-ARETZ ET-HA-YAM W'ET - KAL - ASHER - BAM WA-YANAKH BA-YOM
HA-SHEBIEE AL-KEN BERAK YAHOWAH ET-YOM HA-SHABBAT WAI-QADSHEHU:

כבד את–אביך ואת–אמך למען יארכון ימיך על האדמה

אשר–יהוה אלהיך נתן לך:

5. KABED ET - ABI-KA W'ET-IMEKA LE-MA'AN:
YA'ARIKUN YAMEY-KA AL HA-ADAMAH ASHER-YAHOWAH ELOHAY-KA NOTEN LAK:

לא תרצח:

6. LO TIRTZAKH:

לא תנאף:

7. LO TINAPH:

לו תגנב:

8. LO TIGNOB:

לא–תענה ברעך עד שקר:

9. LO - TA'ANEH BEREA-KA ED SHAQER:

לא תחמד בית רעך לא–תחמד אשת רעך ועבדו ואמתו ושורו

וחמרו וכל אשר לרעך:

10. LO TAKHMOD BAYT RE'EKA LO - TAKHMODE ESHET
RE'EKA W'ABDO WA-AMATO W'SHORO WA-KHAMORO W'KOL ASHER LE-RE'EKA:

TORAH

From H3384; a precept or statute, especially the Decalogue or Pentateuch: - law. Figuratively to point out (as if by aiming the finger), to teach: - (+) archer, cast, direct, inform, instruct.

H8451

"Think not that I am come to destroy the Torah (Law), or the prophets: I am not come to destroy, but to fulfil." -Matthew 5:17

HEBREW/ARAMAIC PRONUNCIATION	ENGLISH TRANSLATION	STRONG'S NUMBER	ANCIENT (PALEO) HEBREW	BIBLICAL HEBREW
TAKHPHENES	TAHPENES	H8472	𐤔𐤍𐤐𐤇𐤕	תַּחְפְּנֵיס

takh-pen-ace'
wife of the king; of Egyptian derivation; *Tachpenes*, an Egyptian woman: - Tahpenes.

| TAMAR | TAMAR | H8558 | 𐤓𐤌𐤕 | תָּמָר |

tâmâr, taw-mawr';
From an unused root meaning to be erect; a palm tree: - palm (tree).

| TAPHATH | TAPHATH | H8297 | 𐤕𐤐𐤈 | טָפַת |

taw-fath'
Probably from H5197; a *dropping* (of ointment); *Taphath*, an Israelitess: - Taphath.

| TIMNA | TIMNA | H8294 | 𐤏𐤍𐤌𐤕 | תִּמְנָע |

tim-naw'
From H4513; *restraint*; *Timna*, the name of two Edomites: - Timna, Timnah.

| TIRTZAH | TIRZAH | H8656 | 𐤄𐤑𐤓𐤕 | תִּרְצָה |

teer-tsaw'
From H7521; *delightsomeness*; *Tirtsah*, a place in Palestine; also an Israelitess: - also an Israelitess: - Tirzah.

| TRUPHASAH | TRYPHOSA | G5173 | 𐤔𐤐𐤅𐤓𐤕 | טְרוּפְסָה |

troo-fo'-sah
From G5172; *luxuriating*; *Tryphosa*, a Christian female: - Tryphosa.

| TRUPHENAH | TRYPHENA | G5170 | 𐤈𐤍𐤅𐤐𐤅𐤓𐤕 | טְרוּפִינָה |

troo'-fahee-nah
From G5172; *luxurious*; *Tryphaena*, a Christian woman: - Tryphena.

| TZERUAH | ZERUAH | H6871 | 𐤏𐤅𐤓𐤑 | צְרוּעָה |

tser-oo-aw'
Feminine passive participle of H6879; *leprous*; *Tseruah*, an Israelitess: - Zeruah.

HEBREW/ARAMAIC PRONUNCIATION	ENGLISH TRANSLATION	STRONG'S NUMBER	ANCIENT (PALEO) HEBREW	BIBLICAL HEBREW
TZERUYAH	ZERUIAH	H6870	ヨΨꓶꓨℸ	צְרוּיָה

tser-oo-yaw'
Feminine participle passive from the same as H6875; *wounded*; *Tserujah*, an Israelitess: - Zeruiah.

| TZIBIYAH | TABITHA *DORCAS | H6646 | ヨΨgꓶ | צִבְיָה |

tseb-ee-yaw';
Feminine of H6643; a female gazelle; in the sense of *prominence*; *splendor* (as *conspicuous*); also a *gazelle* (as *beautiful*): - beautiful (-ty), glorious (-ry), goodly, pleasant.

| TZILLAH | ZILLAH | H6741 | ℥Cꓶ | צִלָּה |

tsil-law'
shade, whether literally or figuratively: - defence, shade (-ow).; *Tsillah*, an antediluvian woman: - Zillah.

| TZIPORAH | ZIPPORAH | H6855 | ℥ꝙꓶℸ | צִפֹּרָה |

tsip-po-raw'
bird, fowl, sparrow; tsipporah, Moses' wife: - Zipporah.

| WASHTI | VASHTI | H2060 | ꓶⵝwℵ | וַשְׁתִּי |

wash-tee';
beautiful; of Persian origin; *Vashti*, the queen of Xerxes: - Washti.

צ TZIPORAH (Sparrow)

YAHOSHUA

From H3068 and H3467; YAHOWAH is salvation; YAHOWAH-saved; Jehoshua (that is, Joshua), the Yisraelim Messiah and only begotton Son of YAHOWAH: - Yahoshua, Yahoshuah, Joshua. Compare H1954, H3442.

<table>
<tr><th>HEBREW/ARAMAIC PRONUNCIATION</th><th>ENGLISH TRANSLATION</th><th>STRONG'S NUMBER</th><th>ANCIENT (PALEO) HEBREW</th><th>BIBLICAL HEBREW</th></tr>
<tr><td>YAHOADAN</td><td>JEHOADDAN</td><td>H3086</td><td>𐤉𐤄𐤅𐤏𐤃𐤍</td><td>יְהוֹעַדָּן</td></tr>
<tr><td colspan="5">yeh-ho-ad-dawn'
From H3068 and H5727; YAHOWAH-pleased; Jehoaddin or Jehoaddan, an Israelitess: - Jehoaddan.</td></tr>
<tr><td>YAHOSHEBA</td><td>JEHOSHEBA</td><td>H3089</td><td>𐤉𐤄𐤅𐤔𐤁𐤏</td><td>יְהוֹשֶׁבַע</td></tr>
<tr><td colspan="5">yeh-ho-sheh'-bah
From H3068 and H7650; YAHOWAH-sworn; Jehosheba, an Israelitess: - Jehosheba. Compare H3090.</td></tr>
<tr><td>YEDIDAH</td><td>JEDIDAH</td><td>H3040</td><td>𐤉𐤃𐤉𐤃𐤄</td><td>יְדִידָה</td></tr>
<tr><td colspan="5">yed-ee-daw'
Feminine of H3039; beloved; Jedidah, an Israelitess: - Jedidah.</td></tr>
<tr><td>YEHUDIYTH</td><td>JUDITH</td><td>H3067</td><td>𐤉𐤄𐤅𐤃𐤉𐤕</td><td>יְהוּדִית</td></tr>
<tr><td colspan="5">yeh-hoo-deeth'
The same as H3066; Jewess; Jehudith, a Canaanitess: - Judith.</td></tr>
<tr><td>YEKALYAH</td><td>JECHOLIAH</td><td>H8472</td><td>𐤉𐤊𐤋𐤉𐤄</td><td>יְכָלְיָה</td></tr>
<tr><td colspan="5">yek-ol-yaw'(-hoo), yek-ee-leh-yaw'
From H3201 and H3050; YAH will enable; Jekoljah or Jekiljah, an Israelitess: - Jecholiah, Jecoliah.</td></tr>
<tr><td>YEMIMAH</td><td>JEMIMA</td><td>H3224</td><td>𐤉𐤌𐤉𐤌𐤄</td><td>יְמִימָה</td></tr>
<tr><td colspan="5">yem-ee-maw'
Perhaps from the same as H3117; properly warm, that is, affectionate; hence dove (compare H3123); Jemimah, one of Job's daughters: - Jemimah.</td></tr>
<tr><td>YERIOTH</td><td>JERIOTH</td><td>H3408</td><td>𐤉𐤓𐤉𐤏𐤅𐤕</td><td>יְרִיעוֹת</td></tr>
<tr><td colspan="5">yer-ee-ohth'
Plural of H3407; curtains; Jerioth, an Israelitess: - Jerioth.</td></tr>
<tr><td>YERUSHAH</td><td>JERUSHAH</td><td>H3388</td><td>𐤉𐤓𐤅𐤔𐤄</td><td>יְרוּשָׁה</td></tr>
</table>

HEBREW/ARAMAIC PRONUNCIATION	ENGLISH TRANSLATION	STRONG'S NUMBER	ANCIENT (PALEO) HEBREW	BIBLICAL HEBREW
yer-oo-shaw', yer-oo-shaw' Feminine passive participle of H3423; *possessed*; *Jerusha* or *Jerushah*, an Israelitess: - Jerusha, Jerushah.				
YOEL	JOEL	H3100	𐤉𐤅𐤀𐤋	יוֹאֵל
yo-ale' From H3068 and H410; *YAHOWAH* (is his) *ELOHIM*; *Joel*, the name of twelve Israelites: - Joel.				
YOKEBED	JOCHEBED	H3115	𐤉𐤅𐤊𐤁𐤃	יוֹכֶבֶד
yo-keh'-bed From H3068 contracted and H3513; *Jehovah-gloried*; *Jokebed*, the mother of Moses: - Jochebed.				
YOKHANAH	JOANNA	G2489	𐤉𐤅𐤇𐤍𐤄	יוֹחָנָה
ee-o-an'-nah From H3068 and H2603; *YAHOWAH-favored*;; *Joanna*, a Christian: - Joanna.				
YULYA	JULIA	G2456	𐤉𐤅𐤋𐤉𐤀	יוּלְיָא
ee-oo-lee'-ah; Feminine of the same as G2457; centurion; Julia, a Messianic woman: - Julia.				
ZEBIDAH	ZEBUDAH	H2080	𐤆𐤁𐤉𐤃𐤄	זְבִידָה
zeb-ee-daw' Feminine from H2064; *giving*; *Zebidah*, an Israelitess: - Zebudah.				
ZERESH	ZERESH	H2238	𐤆𐤓𐤔	זֶרֶשׁ
zeh'-resh gold; of Persian origin; *Zeresh*, Haman's wife: - Zeresh.				
ZILPAH	ZILPAH	H2153	𐤆𐤋𐤐𐤄	זִלְפָּה
zil-paw From an unused root apparently meaning to *trickle*, as myrrh; fragrant *dropping*; *Zilpah*, Leah's maid: - Zilpah.				

YEHUDIYTH

(Jewess)

NOTES

KNOWING OUR H.I.S.TORY

The Hebrew Israelite Story

The Hebrew Israelite Story, H.I.S.tory, is rooted deep in the unspoken and under documented history of the so called Black/Afro-Latino/Native American.

There were many slaves who knew who they were and tried to maintain their heritage in a land that was not theirs. They demonstrated this through artifacts such as the Cursive Hebrew writings on the pews of the First African Baptist Church in Savannah, GA and by leading rebellions with the Bible as their foundation of "Truth."

We Must Remember Our Hebrew Israelite Story And Pass It Down To Future Generations.

Some of the early slaves who possessed the strength of our ancestors were Gabriel Prosser and Nat Turner. They each are reported in history as standing on the word of YAH and using HIS WORD to lead rebellions against those who were the oppressors of our people.

Psalms 9:9
"YAHOWAH also will be a refuge for the oppressed, a refuge in times of trouble."

These gentlemen were some of the first stones of the foundation for those who followed and continued in the study and dissemination of HIS WORD; bringing forth the "TRUTH."

As we continue our journey, though the Hebrew Israelite Story, H.I.S.tory, we enter the era of the Israelites being birthed in America. Some of the first men to acknowledge the so called Black/Afro-Latino/Native American were the Israelites of the Bible were F. S. Cherry, William Saunders Crowdy, Wentworth A. Mathews, Israel ben Newman, Mordecai Herman, and Arnold Josiah Ford Moshe Ben Kareem (MaShah), and Yaiqab Ben Gad. Each of these men started congregations to teach the lost sheep of Israel who they were according the Bible. They are a part of the next level of foundational stones in the Hebrew Israelite Story which paved the way for our current Lions of Judah who are continuing to teach the lost sheep of Israel (Banging on Esau) across the four corners of the earth.

NOTE: "The Mystery Stone" has the 10 Commandments inscribed in Ancient Paleo Hebrew on a stone found by the local native indians in New Mexico at that time. "Though people were aware of the rock when New Mexico became a territory in 1850, no one could read it. Local Indians told the owner of the land in 1871 that the rock predated their tribes coming to the area". http://www.legendsofamerica.com/nm-riopuercovalley.html

We Can All Agree On Keeping The Laws, Statutes, and Commandments of YAHOWAH.

Though all of these groups may have differences in doctrine, we can all agree on keeping the Laws, Statutes, and Commandments of YAHOWAH.

Isaiah 11: 12

And he shall set up an ensign for the nations, and shall assemble the outcasts of Yisra'EL, and gather together the dispersed of Yehudah from the four corners of the earth.

This just a small list of all the Israelites awakened in the last days.

Ambassadors of Christ (AOC)
Army of Israel (AOI)
B'nai Adath
B'nai Zaqen
Banya Yasharahla
Beth ELOHIM
Beth Shalom
Brazilian Israelites
Commandment Keepers
Dimona Israelites
Dominican Israelites
Ethiopian Israelites
For Our People Edification (F.O.P.E.)
Ha'Shabbah
Haitian Israelites
House of David (HOD)
House of Israel (HOI)
I AM ISRAEL (IAI)
Igbo Israelites
Israelite Heritage
Israelite Preparatory Institute (I.P.I.)
Israelite School of Universal Practical Knowledge (ISUPK)
Israelites Scattered in Africa
Israelites Scattered in Asia
Israelites Scattered in Europe
Israelites Scattered in South America
Israelites United in Christ (IUIC)
Jamaican Israelites

KHAI YASHUA
Kol Sheariyth
Light of Zion
Lions of Israel
MYMG
Mexican Israelites
Nation of Israel (NOI)
Native American Israelites
NCCI
NCCI Sanctioned Body
Puerto Rican Israelites
Qahal
Saints of Christ (England)
Sh'ma Yisrael
Shield of Wisdom
Shomrey Ha'Torah
Sicarii
Sounds of Sinai (Tabernacle of ELOHIM)
South American Israelites
Strong Tower
Sword of Zion
Tabernacles of Israel (Jamaica)
The House of the Redeemed Servants
The Path to YAHUAH
United Congregation of Israel
United Kingdom Israelites
United Kingdom of Israel Congregation (UKOIC)
YAH'S House
YAHAWAH'S Camp

Double Honor to all the Israelite Assemblies, Camps, and Congregations spreading the truth throughout the four corners of the earth. Shalom to All of Israel from Brother JediYah Melek

NOTES

NOTES

JediYAH Melek Ben Dani'EL

Khasidah KhaniYAH Melek

YaqarYAH Bat JediYAH Ben Dani'EL

GadelYAH Ben Manassheh Ephraim

Printed in the USA
CPSIA information can be obtained
at www.ICGtesting.com
LVHW070836220224
772216LV00004BA/49